P9-DYO-535

DATE DUE

ON THE HIGH

How to Survive Being Promoted

WIRE

Robert W. Gunn and Betsy Raskin Gullickson

Foreword by James Burke

Westport, Connecticut
London

Library of Congress Cataloging-in-Publication Data

Gunn, Robert W., 1947–
    On the high wire : how to survive being promoted / Robert W. Gunn and Betsy
Raskin Gullickson ; foreword by James Burke.
        p. cm.
    Includes bibliographical references and index.
    ISBN 0-275-98487-7 (alk. paper)
    1. Leadership.   2. Career development.   3. Executive ability.   I. Gullickson,
Betsy Raskin.   II. Title.
    HD57.7.G86 2005
    658.4'092–dc22   2004028178

British Library Cataloguing in Publication Data is Available

Library of Congress Catalog Card Number: 2004028178
ISBN: 0-275-98487-7

First Published in 2005

Praeger Publishers, 88 Post Road West, Westport, CT 06881
An imprint of Greenwood Publishing Group, Inc.
www.praeger.com

Printed in the United States of America

The paper used in this book complies with the Permanent Paper Standard
issued by the National Information Standards Organization (Z39.48–1984).

10   9   8   7   6   5   4   3   2   1

To Brooke and Remy

To Gary

Who hold the net under the wire for us.

Contents

SECOND PRECEPT: STRONG CONNECTIONS BEGIN WITH RESPECT
FOR SEPARATE THINKING

THIRD PRECEPT: THE CALMER YOU BECOME, THE MORE POWERFUL
YOU BECOME—AND THE MORE YOU CAN ACHIEVE

Foreword

Over the many years that I've known Bob Gunn, I've watched him develop as a mentor to emerging managers. And he has challenged me: could I recall a singular inspiration that pointed me on my own path to leadership? What came to mind was a time when I felt sure that I was about to be fired.

Having been hired to create a marketing department for Johnson & Johnson, my first new product had been a colossal flop. But what should be a more natural brand extension for our baby lotion and creams than a chest rub with medicinal vapors for those times when babies fall ill? Wouldn't mothers everywhere use it? The concept had tested well, and early trials had been encouraging.

Unfortunately, I had completely overlooked the details of manufacturing. In order to give the chest rub enough shelf life to withstand the travails of distribution, our engineers could not prevent it from congealing, making it nearly impossible to dispense. Reluctantly, after much trial and error, we threw in the towel and hauled tons of finished product to the landfill. Better than dumping it in the Raritan River, at least.

So now it was time to pay the piper. I had been summoned to the office of the General, Robert Wood Johnson, the legendary chairman of J&J. As I walked into the Georgian building that housed J&J's offices, I was thinking that the General was a class act. To the father of such classic products as Band-Aids and Johnson's Baby Powder, my failure was barely worthy of two minutes of attention. How many other CEOs would take the time to personally fire an underling under such circumstances? I resolved to be gracious myself as I got off the elevator and headed down the long hallway.

As I strode into the General's office, it seemed like his desk was at the other end of a subway tunnel. He stood up as I approached.

"Come over here; I want to see the man who cost me so much money!" he said. "I understand that we had a big, big inventory write-off, not to mention all the wasted time and expense in getting this product developed."

My heart sank. But then he reached over the expanse of mahogany and added, "Let me shake your hand."

What did he just say? I could hardly believe my ears.

"Look, business is a game of risks, of inevitable mistakes," the General expounded. "If we ever become afraid of acting on what we see, then our leadership legacy will fail the company, our customers, and ultimately our employees. I want to let everyone know how I feel about us taking risks by keeping you on." He paused. And then said: "Just don't do it again." Meeting adjourned.

My mind was reeling. But what I learned from the General that day stayed with me. Far more than what a leader says, what he does and how he does it are what people pay attention to. As Bob and his coauthor Betsy Gullickson put it, "Management mastery demands an artful balance of *doing* and *being.*"

Newly minted managers or those few individuals ascending to the highest office—all need confidence in the face of uncertainty, illumination to see the obvious and act on it, and the surefooted ability to behave in ways that their staffs will find inspiring. So many pundits miss the elusive qualities at the heart of inspired and inspiring management. By challenging conventional assumptions, much as Bob challenged me to reflect on what really mattered in my career, *On the High Wire: How to Survive Being Promoted* promises to make an important difference in the lives of those who ask, or are asked, to take on new burdens.

Mistakes, I've found, tend to get more expensive as job responsibilities grow. Now is the time for the fresh perspective on management and leadership that *On the High Wire* provides.

James Burke
Princeton, N.J.
Former Chairman and Chief Executive Officer,
Johnson & Johnson

Preface:
Authors' Perspectives

This book began as a series of conversations among a few leaders who sensed that fulfilling the duties of management requires something beyond the obvious. It was written for all who are feeling their way along the high wire of increasing responsibility. Who have reached the point where what they already know, the skills that got them here, are no longer enough. Who have come to wonder "Is this all there is?" and "Now what?"

Each of us had been propelled into leadership roles rather suddenly, not having planned or expected to take seats of ultimate accountability. Bob started a company; Betsy replaced a business unit director who had become profoundly ill. We felt as if we were taking our teams into uncharted territory and needed to cross a river so wide that we could not see the far shore. Everyone looked to us to plunge off the river's bank, even though we did not know the depth of the water. To take the first steps on a footbridge, dangling hundreds of feet above a gorge. Or to find the narrowest neck of the river, and build a raft to ford it.

Bob's Story: I Am the Thinker of My Fate

The better someone else's idea was, the more I fought against it, using every debating trick in the book. If that failed, I would use the power of my office (being cofounder of one's company does confer power) as the reason to dismiss it. It was a thinking habit of "needing to be right."

I not only believed that my answer was better than anyone else's, but also expected everyone to see things my way. When I was in that mood, people knew that I would jump down their throats if they disagreed with me. My staffers responded, predictably enough, by not thinking for themselves. I was so blinded by ego that the lack of initiative from demonstrably bright people genuinely puzzled me.

At one meeting I berated them: "You are a smart bunch, so why aren't you producing better conceptual materials for clients to use? Most of the slides you are using are ones that I created years ago." The outburst didn't make me feel any better, and it certainly had no effect in the next couple of months.

Then, in a chance conversation, a junior staff member innocently asked me: "How important is it for you to always be right?"

In that moment, the penny dropped. A vivid mental image—of riding a white horse, charging into battle, sword held high, but not one soldier following—made me laugh out loud. At the next staff meeting, I shared this story. Someone in the back of the room shouted out, "Hey, we figured since it is so important for you to always be right that we'd just sit back and let you do all the work!"

This experience helped me to see my thinking in action. I realized that thought is a universal human function from which we create our own "reality." I was not only the "master of my fate," as the poet says, but the thinker of it. That is when I perceived that my righteousness had felt somehow wrong all along.

But what really motivated me to change was becoming a father. I could not help but see that my son was going to learn much more from my example than from anything I could possibly tell him about living life. What shocked me was how carefully my son watched me (and others) and then imitated what he saw. I became uncomfortable with some of my habits at home as well as at work.

At times the process of change was extremely uncomfortable. I vividly re-call feeling as if the skin were being sandblasted off my body as I reexamined one thinking habit after another—worry, fear, looking good.

But the personal price of discomfort seemed like small change compared to the positive impact I could have on my son, and on the people whom I touched as a leader. It was liberating to know that events, circumstances, or other people did not control my course. I noticed that when I was looking for the positive in situations—appreciating other people's creativity, noticing the warmth I felt toward them, or wanting to do my best to help them live up to their talents—then my mind became quiet and confident. And my feelings evoked a productive and energetic tone in others.

When I realized that "I am the thinker of my fate," I reveled in my own happiness and lightheartedness for a good six months. I simply could not believe my good fortune at having found this fundamental truth. Finally, I was awake to the possibilities in life.

In this way I became master of my destiny. And my purpose changed from serving my own ends to serving others.

Betsy's Story: Finding Calm in Chaos

"Allen has AIDS," said Ray, our company president. Having flown in from New York that morning, he had appeared at my door with Allen just moments before. I'd worked with Allen for eight years; we'd been peers and friends before he became office director and my boss. Over the preceding six months, I'd noticed strange behaviors, and I knew that Allen had been in the hospital for a few days the month before. But I wasn't prepared for this. "He has to resign and will be leaving on Thursday. Will you take over for him?"

My friend is dying, I thought, and reached for his hand. His doctor had advised that if Allen did not reduce his stress, he would be dead by summer. He was one month shy of his 40th birthday.

Now, unsuspecting employees and clients would have to grapple with the shock of losing Allen's charisma, enthusiasm, inspiration. They would need reassurance that the business would continue, that someone would keep them steady.

I had not aspired to run the office, had looked askance at the stress that was involved even in good times. And these were not good times. Having shrunk by a third during the recession of the previous two years, the operation was scrambling to meet income and profit goals. Staff and systems urgently needed to be upgraded. Some of the most talented people were disgruntled and ready to bolt.

But under these circumstances, I could not hesitate. Of course, I would do whatever I could.

The two men left my office. I put my head down on the table and wept, went home that night and wept again as I shared with my husband grief for Allen, and inevitable anxiety.

Thursday morning, the staff assembled. The company chairman spoke first. Immediately, there were gasps and tears. Allen spoke next, poignantly. And then it was my turn. What amazed me was how rock-sure I felt in that moment. Personal insecurities paled beside the needs of the 45 people who now looked to me. As I focused on them, words came easily and clearly, neither rushed nor hesitant.

Three fundamental lessons emerged over the next six months.

My style had been to try to control everything; now, the job was too big. Not only did I find appreciation for others' ability to grow, but also relief at not having to rely solely on my own experience.

I was a champion second-guesser. Now, decisions came so fast and so frequently that I hadn't time to agonize over each one. That meant having to accept inevitable mistakes and then to find the way to make them right. I found liberation from perfectionism.

Most important, in place of worry over how I looked, I focused on building the confidence of the people around me. By putting self-interest in the backseat, I gained a clear connection to inner resources that helped me to keep my bearings and to find calm in chaos.

Our Promise

We've been shaping and testing our perspectives during a combined total of more than 60 years in management. We find our own insights not from intellectual understanding, but rather in the actual living of leadership.

As we've traveled our paths, the people on our teams have begun to laugh more. At times, we see insight flash across their faces, or their shoulders seem to relax, indicating the lightening of their emotional load. Our endeavors have not been perfect, but many of our team members have said, "We think it's the best place we have ever worked." A few have told us that things we've said or experiences we've shared have given them new perspective. We hope that is true for many more that we will never hear from or know about.

But we are quite certain that they have already given us more. Thanks to their candor, we've seen more in and about ourselves. Thanks to their openness to us, we've opened ourselves to new insights and greater wisdom. Thanks to their faith in our leadership, we've bolstered our faith in the unknown. We are profoundly grateful for their tolerance of our shortcomings, their patience when we have lost our bearings, and their compassion in giving us a hand when we are struggling.

In large part, this book is our way of honoring our own commitment to stay on the high wire with ever-deeper levels of security, willpower, and humility. For it is in the process of reflecting and sharing about the fundamental questions that we learn, also.

It is only with the heart that one can see rightly;
What is essential is invisible to the eye.

—Antoine de Saint Exupery, *The Little Prince*

Robert Gunn
Princeton, New Jersey

Betsy Gullickson
Kentfield, California

Acknowledgments

We'd like to express our gratitude to and appreciation for:

- Alexander Caillet, cofounder of Prescient Leaders, who inspires us daily by the passion he brings to improving the global workplace and whose gift for illuminating complex concepts helped us sharpen key points;
- Nick Philipson, our editor, an extraordinary advocate for the reader, whose thoughtful prodding and rigor made this book strong and clear;
- John Willig, our agent, who helped us find our voice and our focus;
- Louis Patler, who set us on the path toward publication;
- Ken Manning, who provided perceptive feedback, grounded in his own experience—as psychologist, coach, and trainer—in developing managers and leaders;
- Gary Gullickson and Brooke Gunn, our spouses, who patiently walked through multiple iterations, adding perspectives from their own work in psychology research and counseling and in childhood development.

We are also grateful to our clients, whose experiences put to the test the ideas in this book. Their courage and commitment to be better managers and leaders teach us on an ongoing basis.

And we appreciate the loyal readers of the columns that we coauthor for *Strategic Finance* magazine, published by the Institute of Management Accountants (IMA), Montvale, N.J., www.strategicfinancemag.com, or www.imanet.org. Some material in this book is adapted, with permission, from those columns.

INTRODUCTION

Stepping into the Unknown

Key question: I've been promoted to a job and taken on responsibilities that demand abilities different from what got me here. Now what?

Revolution was accomplished gracefully—without rancor, struggle, or bitterness—in Dow Chemical's Human Resources (HR) Department. They reduced headcount by 40%, cut costs by nearly 50%, and restructured so that 60% of the staff had new jobs.

Larry Washington was the executive who made that happen. Nearly five years after he initiated new procedures, Larry's direct reports sustained an infectious enthusiasm for improving the HR department's contribution to the company.

Such achievement—making a lasting difference—is every newly promoted manager's dream. But at the moment we make decisions, we are committing ourselves—and those who follow us—to a course of action with an uncertain outcome. We are, in a sense, stepping out on the high wire.

There comes a moment at the circus when all heads turn toward the center ring. High above the sawdust floor, a spotlight picks out a slender figure standing on a cramped platform. Eyes focused on some distant point, the performer places one slippered foot and then the next on an impossibly thin wire. He glides slowly at first, then picks up speed, tipping and dipping a long pole in a struggle for balance. There is no place to hide. Any misstep hurts; it may even be fatal.

The experience of the newly appointed manager can be just as breathtaking. Assuming an increasing share of responsibility has a bit of mystery attached to it. A person does a good job, makes a solid contribution based on individual effort, and wins promotion. Or circumstances shift, thrusting the manager forward. Knowledge, talent, and experience add up to success and new challenges.

The step up from "one of the guys" to boss may seem as facile as a congratulatory e-mail. But sooner or later we bump into a transition in which we cannot rely on the behaviors that have worked for us before. We feel an ineffable itch, the uneasy sense that we are missing something.

Can't see the far side. Mustn't go back. Won't climb down. Don't dare even to look: is there, invisible in the dark beneath the wire, a safety net?

The High Wire

Before: One of the Guys	Stepping Up: Boss
Do-er	Delegator
"In the trenches"	"30,000 ft." perspective
Managing projects	Leading people
Measured by personal performance	Measured by group success

The Uneasy Transition

Very possibly you find yourself on such a high wire, too. Perhaps your knowledge and experience have propelled you into a role where you are seeking ways to perform that are sustainable and energy giving, rather than exasperating or tiring.

Conceivably, you feel a bit uncomfortable—maybe even discouraged. You may believe that no one can have a lasting and positive influence on an organization. The price of managing may seem too high when measured against the quality of your personal life; too many of the available role models seem harsh, distant, or isolated.

But what if you could transcend the arrogance, negativity, or busyness that we so often associate with management and leadership?

What if you could inspire a team to accomplish more than they dreamed—without burning themselves out?

What if it were possible for the management burden to be lightened?

What if the so-called personal price of being a manager were zero?

Such questions demand unconventional answers. No longer can organizations afford to be seduced by the charismatic hero—who charges in and churns up great change, but leaves the field littered with bodies. Nor can institutions survive if managers are wedded to the past: heads buried deeply in the sand, ignoring a world where customers assess performance globally and expect more value in every new transaction.

The spotlight must turn to a different kind of manager: steadfast, open, reflective. Men and women who evoke confidence and trust. Who achieve the results that the insatiable market demands without destroying the people that make up the company. Who balance undaunted drive with values.

What's the secret that these managers know?

Earned Capabilities Plus Innate Capacity—Not Just the Doing, but the *Being* of a Manager

Larry, whom we met at the start of this chapter, was able to be a leader of graceful revolution partly by drawing on 25 years of experience at Dow, in a sequence of positions that gave him a comprehensive understanding of the organization. Accumulated knowledge—*earned capabilities*—created a foundation that enabled him to assemble the right team, to instill confidence in that team, and to frame profound questions.

But Larry's leadership added important, *innate capacity*: not only did he know what to *do;* he also had a sense of how to *be.* Larry (1) had a desirable outcome clearly in mind, but (2) he made no effort to dictate what steps to take, just (3) asked questions and kept his mind open to the emerging wisdom of the team. Above all, he showed up in a way that encouraged the team to work in a positive, calm frame of mind—meetings never went on too long; difficult decisions were not rushed; everyone was treated with respect.

Both innate capacity and earned capability are valuable management assets. Capability represents knowledge honed by experience. Because it is tangible and measurable, capability is traditionally easier to reward. Capacity is the inner game of managing, of being able to see the obvious and do it. It taps an intelligence that is available 24/7. Like Larry, managers who know how to achieve standout results rely not just on their earned capabilities, but also on their innate capacity for inspiring and motivating others.

The value of capability includes its role in shortcutting decisions; we don't have to reinvent the wheel if we know something that has worked before. But that's just the beginning. In the ongoing evolution of managers into leaders, the importance of experience is that it can enable us to explore ever-deeper questions.

Furthermore, without some base of knowledge—some capability—our innate capacity cannot fully engage. Consider two people watching a rising sun paint the sky in brilliant shades of red. Both have the capacity to notice and to be moved—perhaps catching their breath at the sheer beauty of the scene. But the one who has training and experience as a sailor knows, "Red sky at night, sailor's delight; red sky in the morning, sailor take warning." Thus, she has the capability of reading the warning signs of bad weather and then taking steps to prepare. She uses both capability and capacity to keep herself and her team safe.

Knowledge and other forms of capability are acquired and individual. Insight and other forms of capacity are innate and universal. Together, they make a virtuous circle at the core of inspired and inspiring management.

Capability provides the tools that allow us to use our capacity, to put our inborn wisdom and creativity to the service of our aspirations. And capacity gives the security to acknowledge which capabilities we need to strengthen or to supplement. Management becomes a thing of beauty when experience is seasoned with insight—capability in service of expanded capacity.

Looking for the Invisible

> Bob D'Alessandri, vice president of The Health Sciences Center at West Virginia University, is one of the longest-tenured medical school deans in the country. He recounts that when he became dean, some 15 years ago, someone gave him this bit of advice: "Seeing the invisible is the true ability of all leaders." That simple statement struck home. Dean D'Alessandri taped it underneath the glass atop his desk, and he tried to follow it for years.
>
> But he assumed that "the invisible must be out there, somewhere. If I keep looking, sooner or later I'll find it." After one particularly trying day, he realized: "I was looking the wrong way. The 'invisible' is that which is in me; not just for me, alone, but within every human being." He saw, for the first time, that understanding human functioning—the capacity to find answers by looking within—was the first step to unleashing potential for himself and then, surely, in the institution.

Management, like any game, happens in the moment, usually unscripted. Heads snap to see how the boss will respond to the unexpected. Employees read every clue, mimic the smallest idiosyncrasy. They notice and appreciate the manager who has the unerring ability to say or do exactly what the moment calls for.

But the external behaviors are not where the really important action takes place. Rather, on the inside a gut feeling takes hold; a sense of knowing swims into consciousness. The manager says or does something perfectly right, and the organization moves forward, makes progress, releases human potential.

Skillful managers, like superior athletes, understand the value of practice to improve their earned capabilities. But in the game they drop conscious effort and rely most on instinct, on innate capacity. That's what's called, "playing in the zone."

The Exhilaration of Exploration

To lead a team, you must help the group keep its bearings and achieve success in the face of large opportunities and obstacles. Since institutions accomplish work through collective energy, leaders need to ensure that exploration has a purpose. In other words, leaders begin the journey by clearly articulating a goal.

In 1961, when President John F. Kennedy challenged the nation to put a man on the moon by the end of that decade, the requisite technology was mere theory. The goal's achievement, in 1969, resulted from people creatively taking one step after another towards this huge challenge.

Within that singular purpose there had to be room for exploration; "mucking around" is an element critical to progress. When a team is looking to do something uncommon, they are inevitably going to take wrong turns and follow false leads. Mistakes teach us where the right path lays. "Living your life in fear that you're going to do it wrong," says author and Zen teacher Cheri Huber, "is like an explorer who is afraid of getting lost."[1]

In essence, we are suggesting that great achievements are possible only when we drop our fanatic dependence on accumulated knowledge, and that can be very difficult. But as an oft-quoted Chinese proverb says: "Insanity is doing the same thing in the same way and expecting a different result." New solutions, new approaches require fresh thinking—in other words, insight.

Every human being has an inborn capacity for insight. But some people seem to have a knack for it. What's their secret? They know that tapping insight requires us to release ourselves from the mental prison of egocentric thinking—hard to do when people have self-esteem at stake, but easy when we are not thinking only about ourselves.

High-Wire Investigation

Conventional: Debate	Step Up: Connection
"My right answer"	"I don't know"
Agree/disagree	"What's new here?"
Right/wrong	Grain of truth
Good/bad	Points of view
Yes/no	"What if?"
"Solve it myself"	Collaboration

Leading is...

A form of taking action...stimulated by our insights about what appears obvious, directed by the process of reflection about the important questions, and guided by the learning that comes via exploration.

To foster the spirit of investigation, we must step back from our own "right answers." We must break out of the mode of "two-way thinking"—critically assessing what others say from the standpoint of debate: agree/disagree, right/wrong, yes/no, good/bad. When we listen reflectively, we create the kind of dialogue in which people see a third, even a fourth and fifth, possibility. We—and they—are able to integrate seemingly conflicting points of view, taking the best ideas and putting them to work in novel ways.

Columbo, the detective played by Peter Falk in the old TV series, was our kind of hero. Unconcerned about whether he looked stupid, he would pose seemingly innocuous questions, solicit another character (usually his prime suspect) to "help him out," and generally just play dumb. He assumed naiveté, which deflected the defensiveness that is provoked by positional authority. Above all, he maintained an open mind, which prevented him from jumping to conclusions prematurely. And despite Columbo's rumpled, fumbling demeanor, he was ultimately effective because he was truly curious.

In other words, a manager should be like an explorer, motivating people to continually try new things because they sense that there are possibilities beyond what they already know. Skillful managers foster feelings of curiosity to help people let go of negative thoughts and free their minds. We boldly lead our team into the unknown future not because of past success, but because we are eager to see what new possibilities will appear.

We stare down fear, like the high-wire walker who feeds on the thrill of the crossing. While her feet touch the wire, her spirit connects to the audience and to the only net she really needs—an inner sureness. She remains, paradoxically, grounded—no matter how high the wire. Similarly, every manager can rely on the invisible capacity that is always present.

Look up from what you already know. There's a different way to walk the high wire.

What Lies Beyond What You Already Know...A Map to the High Wire

Come to this book curious to explore beyond the conventional beliefs about management. As you move through the following chapters, you'll find answers to key questions:

First Precept: Masterful Managers Artfully Balance Doing and Being

1. Grace in Change: How do I effect change, keeping my bearings and hewing to my values even as I drive for results?
2. The Productivity Paradox: How can I—and my team—avert burnout while achieving standout results?
3. Creativity and Strategy: Creativity and strategic thinking seem to belong to an anointed few. Can I find those talents in myself?
4. Better Decisions: How can I act from a sense of *knowing* my decisions are sound, inspiring confidence in others, as well?
5. Letting Go To Get Ahead: As I transition from doing to delegating, how do I inspire others to achieve goals using their own skill and ingenuity?

Second Precept: Strong Connections Begin with Respect for Separate Thinking

6. Job One—Setting the Right Tone: How do I create feelings of enthusiasm *and* get the nitty-gritty tasks accomplished?
7. Sales and Meetings: How can I ensure that interpersonal relationships become stronger so that I can meet goals?
8. Teams—Working As One: Too many teams take too much time to do too little. How can I harness collective energy effectively?
9. Managing Conflicts: How can I accommodate conflicts so that they energize my team, rather than provoking resistance and resentment?
10. Employee Relations: How do I handle difficult conversations and performance problems, saying what needs to be said without making things go from bad to worse?

Third Precept: The Calmer You Become, the More Powerful You Become—and the More You Can Achieve

11. Focus and Clarity: As I move from working in the trenches to framing the big picture, what thinking patterns do I need to change? And how?

12. The Antidote to Stress: Must I invest heroic amounts of energy to motivate others and gain recognition? Must I sacrifice home, family, friends to succeed?

13. Measuring Up: Now that the stakes are higher, how should I be evaluated?

14. The Wellspring: How can I sustain energy and stay balanced in the face of limitless demands on my time?

Afterword: Why Lead?

Is the effort to walk the wire worth it?

Greatness is a road leading towards the unknown.

—General Charles deGaulle,
late Prime Minister of France[2]

FIRST PRECEPT

Masterful Managers Artfully Balance Doing and Being

CHAPTER 1

Grace in Change

Key question: How do I effect change, keeping my bearings and hewing to my values even as I drive for results?

Eddie Montana did not want to be in this meeting. He could not stop fidgeting and actually paced around the conference room even while his boss was mid-presentation. Eddie's nervous energy was the physical manifestation of his emotional discomfort with the executive's request: Eddie and Alcoa's other regional sales heads had to work together to figure out which staff members would have their jobs eliminated. Costs had to be cut, and quickly.

Eddie had always gotten results by asking people for their loyalty in exchange for his support. Indeed, reciprocity—"You look out for me, and I'll look out for you"—was his core value. He'd do virtually anything to help his team succeed, and they loved him for it. In return, he expected them to be loyal, just as he gave his own loyalty to the company.

But, now, his organization was going to be downsized. Even worse: Eddie would not be able to exercise unilateral power about who was going to be laid off. His authority to deliver on the implied promise of loyalty had been stripped away. What leverage would he have now? What was he supposed to do? Stall for time? Convince his peers that his people were better? Work the boss off-line? Instinctively, Eddie knew that these time-honored tactics would backfire; the executive meant business, and he was going to hold the regional managers to account.

Back and forth went Eddie's thoughts, matching his nervous pacing. The harder he tried to find a way to stick by his employees, the more frightened he got. Suddenly, Eddie was jolted to stillness. A calm feeling swept over him as his thinking stopped momentarily. He had to admit there were problems in the sales organization. So what was he staying loyal *to?*

Eddie turned an objective eye on his team. He realized that a few of his people were actually coasting. They had apparently figured out that *looking* loyal might matter more than what work they accomplished. Obvious, perhaps, to an outsider, but that insight hit Eddie right in the gut.

So he found himself speaking up: "Let's involve our very best salespeople in determining who should be terminated. They are closer to the action and probably have better insights than we do about who is really contributing and who isn't." The moment the words were spoken, Eddie felt confident. He knew that he would end up with a stronger organization and keep the loyalty of the people who were most critical for his success.

Eddie had found a way to sustain what really mattered in the face of change. A positive outcome became possible when Eddie had that shift in thinking that quelled his anxiety, and his thoughts stopped racing. He was then able to disentangle assumptions from values. And to see new potentials.

In short, he overcame the single biggest obstacle to balancing values and exigencies: mental paralysis engendered by fear.

Coping in the Void

To put it simply, change means that we are driving into the unknown. You can see the yearning for some sort of guarantee whenever an organization faces significant change. The bigger the change, the more ominously the decisions loom in people's minds. Everyone anticipates that things will be different from what they have known, but they don't know *how* different.

While we may be convinced that the chosen direction is right, the outcomes can never be proven in advance. Imagination fills the void; and when it combines with insecurity, it generates painful, if not crippling, doubts and concerns.

Must change be as difficult as a high-wire act? Yes, says conventional wisdom. Typical is a speech given in 2002 by the CEO of a Fortune 500 company. Exhorting his organization to become a "top performer," he urged employees to take risks, to solve problems without waiting to be told what to do, and to "give a damn" about their customers.[1] These are all laudable goals.

But the CEO assumed that change had to be imposed on the organization. Even though he acknowledged that no one can force others to change against their will, he urged managers to cast overboard those who did not "get it"—whatever "it" was—and to gear up for a protracted effort to reinvent the organization.

What this CEO failed to see was that his very thoughts about achieving the desired transformation made it all the more difficult to accomplish. By saying that it would be hard, he created anxiety. By underscoring that not everyone would make it, he created fear. By expressing outcomes in fuzzy jargon, he caused confusion.

Like this CEO, many managers start from misguided perspectives. They work from the assumption that people will not step up to the actions implied by the big decisions. Believing that change must be force-fed, they launch massive programs to drive new behaviors. They invest mightily to generate slogans, incentives, task forces, and meetings—sometimes to aim merely for the most modest shift in direction.

When we see one of these juggernauts taking shape, we grow very skeptical. They generally accomplish far less than their original promise; within a few years little, if any, evidence may remain of their impact.

Changing Our Minds

In other words, too many change initiatives place far too much emphasis on the mechanics of the process without appreciating that change is something we do virtually every moment. Indeed, as the Greek philosopher Heraclitis said, "Nothing endures but change." That is certainly true in the natural world: seasons turn; continents move; galaxies form and revolve; stars burn out. We once saw a time-lapse movie of Cape Cod's shoreline over the past 500 years. The coast grew, shrank, and shifted as the tides moved the sand (proving the folly of building your dream house on any beach!).

People change naturally, too. Are you the same person today that you were 20 years or even two years ago? Reflecting on our past gives us vivid flashbacks of certain events, but we can scarcely recall what it felt like to be "us." Who are those kids captured in school photos and home movies, or by yellowing term papers? Those days seem as remote as our imaginings of the future did when we were young. Are we merely making up some of those memories, or did they really happen?

We continually learn, adapt, even transform the tenor of our lives. That we do this is so obvious that it scarcely needs comment. But the power behind our ability to change may be overlooked or taken for granted. And that is our innate mental capacity. We shape our lives—by choice or on autopilot—from our thoughts as they flow, one after another (figure 1.1).

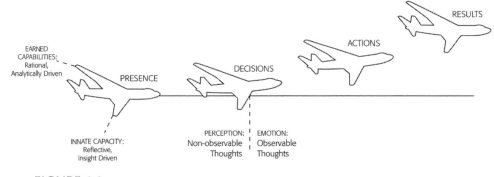

FIGURE 1.1

Balance and integration of earned capabilities and innate capacity is essential on "life's flight path." As we start down the runway to experience, our perceptions—our thoughts—are invisible to others, and often obscure even to us. Emotions—moods—are often easier to observe, helping us to become aware of our thoughts. The more aware we are, the more choice we have: whether or not to "take off" with decisions that lead to actions and generate the results that we then call "my life."

Why is it so hard to change? Because we operate from a set of assumptions. These unexamined thoughts provoke feelings that lead to certain behaviors with specific results. The challenge for a manager is to "see" the invisible link between her own thoughts and her behaviors—and then to realize that, as humans, all of us function fundamentally the same way.

Becoming conscious of our *feelings* gives us the awareness to notice if our *thinking* is helping us achieve the results we desire. And because we are our own creative agents, able to use our thoughts intentionally, we have the power to change outcomes by entertaining new thoughts.

Stay Out of the Trap of Past Success

Glen was a sales wiz at his former company. He had a natural ability to negotiate big, complicated deals artfully and always with an eye to the interests of his employer. He prided himself that no client could ever take advantage of him in a negotiation.

But Glen faced a whole new game when he became VP of Sales at a company that was pioneering a brand new market—HR outsourcing. Prospective clients assumed that Glen's team knew much more than they did and could easily take advantage of their ignorance. But Glen, working from assumptions formed from his previous experience, still believed that the clients had him at a disadvantage.

Needless to say, prospective client meetings were painful. Both sides revealed as little as they could to protect their own perceived vulnerabilities instead of admitting that "no one knew," and they would just have to figure it out together.

Glen was firmly stuck in an old paradigm, hanging on for dear life as the storm called "Uncertainty" raged around him. A series of sales calls went nowhere, but Glen never saw that he was undone by something as simple as a thought habit. It took someone with fresh perspective to sign the first $1 billion HR outsourcing agreement.

The Danger in Playing It Safe

A newly promoted manager is particularly vulnerable to his old thinking habits. After all, these have served him well; that knowledge and experience stored in his brain got him promoted! But when we lack the strength or courage to change our minds—to admit that relying on yesterday's good answer may not work for today's challenge, or that something different might be better than what we've known—we become stuck.

Complicating the issue is the tendency to confuse beliefs and assumptions—which should be continually reassessed as new information becomes available—with values, which are fundamental and transcendent. That's what happened to Eddie at the start of this chapter. A more famous example stems from the early days of the Ford Motor Company. It had achieved dominance by mass-producing the Model T—one model in one color. "You can have any color you want," the saying went, "so long as it's black." Ford's initial success validated its founding principle: "Not wandering from our own path, but doing one thing well."

As times and tastes changed, Henry Ford's stubborn attachment to the black Model T threatened to bankrupt his company. Unwittingly, he was trying to shape a future with too much reliance on an old answer. Was "black" a value? Or was it just an old *belief/assumption* about what it would take to deliver Ford's real *value:* "unless the Company can keep wages high and prices low, it will destroy itself; for otherwise it limits the number of its customers"?[2]

What eventually saved the company was Ford's courage to free his thinking from the past and to take bold action. He shut down production for more than a year and re-tooled. Ford embraced a better way; he embraced change.

Great Outcomes Demand Bold Decisions

But is there any other choice? Do we ever really know what is going to happen from one minute to the next? In truth, we live in and with the unknown all the time.

Sustaining some sense of control seems so important that we try to foster a feeling of security. We wrap ourselves inside predictions—which are nothing but the use of memory and projection to create the illusion that we can *know* the future. Plans, assumptions, predictions, expectations—we move into change as if such thoughts were protective armor. But even the weightiest thoughts cannot keep us safe. Indeed, they may exhaust us.

So if he can't control the future, how can the manager move the team past fear of the unknown? We've learned to think of fear as a stop sign. Does that tell you to stop *forever*: set the emergency brake, park at that spot, furnish and decorate your car, marry and raise a family there? Hardly. The stop sign says: "Heads up! You're at a place where a lot can happen. Be alert. Look around. Pay careful attention. Then proceed with great awareness of what's going on around you."

High-Wire Change Management

Conventional: Don't Lose	Step Up: Win
Focus on sacrifices	Focus on possibilities
"What might go wrong?"	"What needs to go right?"
Anxious	Accepting
Force-feeding	Enrolling
Looking for guarantees	Unfazed by discomfort

By its very nature, the unknown evokes unsettled feelings (figure 1.2). Discomfort may tempt managers to play the game so as not to lose, rather than to win. This insecure mindset biases decision tools and methodologies toward conservatism. It causes us to use assumptions that give more weight to negatives— "what might go wrong"—than to positives—"what needs to go right."

But bold decisions are the precursors of great outcomes. Precisely because the future is unknowable, you may not be able to tell if positive or negative outcomes are more or less likely. It's a bit like what the movie character, Forrest Gump, says: "Life is like a box of chocolates; you never know what you are going to get." With each step up, you assume greater responsibility for maintaining balance—no matter what comes out of the box.

The Newly Promoted Manager's Golden Hour

The need for alertness in the face of change is particularly poignant for newly promoted managers. We all step up to new responsibility with a desire to make a difference; yet we discover that the opportunity to effect real change dwindles with each passing moment.

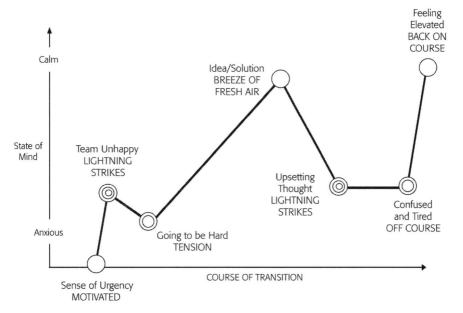

FIGURE 1.2

The normal flow of thoughts and moods is intensified by the insecurity that attends change. It's easier to keep things on course when we stay calm and confident.

What's happening is comparable to what the medical profession calls "The Golden Hour." When someone is injured or suffers a stroke or heart attack, there is a short window of time in which treatment interventions—even small ones—can make a huge difference in ultimate outcomes. Ideally, emergency treatment should begin within 60 minutes: the Golden Hour.

The appointment of a new manager is like a medical event in that it breaks the routine functioning of the organization. Employees are shaken up, negatively or positively; as a result, they are *expecting* something different. There's a brief Golden Hour, during which it's relatively easy to gain support, or at least interest, for new approaches. The effect is short-lived, so the alert manager makes the most of the opportunity to make necessary changes.

The key to the Golden Hour is, first, skilled assessment: knowing what "symptoms" to look for, and what they mean. Of course, the newly appointed manager looks at the obvious—records of work output, personnel files, and so on. Even more important, however, she listens not just to what her new team says, but also for the underlying feeling or tone.

Then she identifies the two or three steps—often, small changes—that can make the greatest immediate difference. As we've seen in the Introduction, she may draw on her earned capabilities: for example, streamlining procedures with systems that have worked for her before. But she must also draw on her innate capacity, applying her wisdom to change the perspective of her team.

In other words, for the new manager, the Golden Hour begins inside her own mind. She listens reflectively for insights to speed learning her new job. But also to see what *isn't* there: what new actions will help the organization shake off the shackles of complacency that virtually all fall prey to when not much new is happening, and things are going well.

The Power of Wonder Grounded in Values

In the past four years Alice has been promoted three times to new locations, serving as the project leader for her company's biggest client, then as the manager of the largest operating center—responsible for people she has never met and operations she did not know much about. Not only has she turned around problem units, she has built a lasting legacy: those businesses have continued to perform well after she has moved on. And she has managed to accomplish these feats with very few personnel changes.

Alice's secret? First, she approached each new assignment with a sense of wonder, of looking to learn. When she took her current position, her predecessor told her that everything was working like the proverbial Swiss watch. And for her first few days on the job, work seemed to go swimmingly. Then Alice bumped into one of the client's vice presidents who made an off-hand comment about how hard it was to get answers from the service center she was running. That caught her attention.

"Hmmm, I wonder what's going on," Alice thought. Later that day, she stopped by the desk of one of the operators and inquired, "Sue, can you show me the oldest open service ticket you have in queue?" Sue made a few keystrokes, and up popped a window with tickets dating back nearly six weeks. The performance standard was 48 hours or less!

Equally important, that performance was contrary to Alice's deeply held values—her insistence on people doing their best, of working for the good of the customer, and of treating each other with respect. Her stance of wonder grounded in values helped Alice see what specific changes could make the greatest difference.

Everyone can be this kind of manager. Changing habits or old behaviors is a capacity all humans possess. The process may not be easy, but it is simple:

1. Tap into your inborn wisdom and common sense by considering the significant questions with a calm mind.

2. Notice and record your insights, which alter perceptions.

3. Adopt new behaviors; practice them consciously, over and over, until they become familiar—a new habit.

High-Wire Key to Keeping Bearings:
Rely on *Inner* Resources

What enables us to stay true to our values while facing change is something not usually talked about in the business context. And that is *faith*. Normal practice is to avoid that word in favor of less religiously loaded terms, such as confidence or trust. But, in truth, sooner or later, all leaders find themselves acting on faith.

By faith, we mean having certainty or conviction about something for which there is no proof. In business we often call this "going on gut instinct." The bigger the idea or decision, the more faith plays a role. Life, unlike a book, simply doesn't allow us to flip to the last page and know how the story will turn out. We have to let things unfold.

Part of faith is trusting our earned capabilities—knowing that we have our whole lives to draw on. This is not our first breath, not the first beat of our heart. However dysfunctional we may sometimes feel, we have learned lessons. We do not walk into the unknown alone; we have with us all of our experiences, all of our life's lessons to remind us that we can prevail.

But, as we have seen in the introduction, we also have the innate capacity to access resources that we cannot see: common sense or wisdom that is somehow greater than our accumulated knowledge. When we have pulled every lever that we can think of and are shocked to stillness, what lies waiting for us is faith. It encourages us to put one foot forward and then the next and the next.

That is faith (or, if you prefer, gut instinct)—not a sweeping religious concept, just keeping on with a sense that, somehow, everything will work out. Whatever mistakes we fall prey to, we'll be able to find a way to make things right—without having to sacrifice what really matters to us.

> Nothing worth doing can be completed in our lifetime,
> Therefore, we must be saved by hope.
> Nothing true or beautiful makes complete sense,
> Therefore, we must be saved by faith.
>
> —Reinhold Niebuhr,
> American religious and social thinker

CHAPTER 2

The Productivity Paradox

Key question: How can I—and my team—avert burnout while achieving standout results?

Carrie was one of those dedicated workers. Night after night, she would stay late at her desk, wrestling with complex assignments. When her boss would urge Carrie to leave early—say, 6:30 P.M.—she would shrug him off. She would drag herself home at 10:30 P.M., then be back at the computer, red-eyed and shoulders sagging, first thing the next morning.

Yes, Carrie was dedicated. Look how hard she was trying! But no one was surprised when she announced that she was quitting.

Carrie could see no other choice. She couldn't recognize that she pushed herself to the point of diminishing returns—that juncture where increased effort returns less and less benefit. What Carrie's boss tried to point her toward was the way to break the cycle: table the subject and engage in something else until you can return with a fresh perspective.

Too many of us are like Carrie. We feel compelled to be more productive. But it seems that the only aspect of productivity that we can control is the *input*—increasingly measured by hours spent on the job. We assume that greater input—that is, more effort, more time—will increase *output*. We are missing the essence of what being productive really means: increasing the value of outputs *while consuming fewer and fewer inputs*. True productivity is sustained when we do things the best way we know how today and invest in continuous improvement for tomorrow. Inputs decline as the work becomes easier, and outputs rise as outcomes become more valuable.

> Not long ago, reported the *New York Times*, a mother was putting her eight-year-old to bed the evening before a school holiday when the child asked, "Mommy, will you have time to play with me tomorrow?" The mother replied, "Honey, I'm so far behind at work that Daddy is going to have to be with you, instead." The child cried out, "But, Mommy, you've been working since before I was born. Aren't you caught up yet?"

As the "80-20 rule" suggests: 80% of results stem from 20% of effort.[1] In other words, our most significant accomplishments result from just a few decisions or actions. Yet most of us wear our busyness like a badge of honor.

Technology, which was supposed to free us, has in some ways made things worse. The response time between request and action has shrunk dramatically thanks to overnight delivery services, electronic distribution, and instant information. Video- and teleconference services allow us to "meet" without even shaking hands. We are accessible by cell phones, pagers, Blackberries, e-mail, and voice mail, 24/7. Since we *can* work anytime, anywhere, it feels like we *must*. Some unfinished task, some unreturned call, some message lurking in cyberspace is always waiting to take your next free moment.

Performance vs. "Performativity"

Paradoxically, the harder we try, the less likely we are to succeed. The more pressure we put on ourselves, the less we act with common sense. The longer our to-do list, the more distracted we are—and the easier it is to put off tackling it. The more we worry, the further the obvious answer slips away from us. The more upset we become, the more difficult it is to see a situation clearly and to make adjustments.

Suppose, for example, your boss asks you to ferret out the answer to a vital question. You automatically respond that you will have it done by tomorrow morning. Then you remember a report that is due, your kid's soccer game, and a scheduled afternoon meeting. In a heartbeat, keenness turns to fret. Anxiety increases the heaviness of the burden but does nothing to get anything done.

Of course, we all want to look good to the boss, to win her applause. A word we've heard applied to this phenomenon by some executive coaches is *performativity*.[2] Performativity, in this context, connotes the urge to do and say things that make us look good, based on what we *assume* to be expected or admired performance. It is a habit of behaving as if we are playing to an unseen audience—one that may, at any moment, hold up cards that score us: so much for technical difficulty, so much for artistic impression. And you just never know what score you're going to get from the Romanian judge!

In other words, performativity is the ego's playground. When we click into performativity, we are protecting or attempting to burnish our self-image. But it's cruelly self-defeating; the more we worry about how others view our performance, the less access we have to the inner resources that can help us the most.

For example, it seems that the most dangerous item in a health club may be the mirror. A recent study at Canada's McMaster University found that exercising in front of a mirror may *de*motivate women to the extent that they won't exercise. Researchers asked 58 sedentary young women about their attitudes toward their bodies and their moods—once as a baseline, then twice more, one week apart, after the women had ridden an exercise bike for 20 minutes. When the women could watch themselves in the mirror, they wound up feeling worse—less calm and more fatigued—than when the mirrors were covered so they couldn't see themselves. Other studies validate that looking into a mirror starts people thinking not just about their physical imperfections, but also about other presumed flaws. Kathleen Martin Ginis, associate professor of health and exercise psychology at McMaster, told the Associated Press: "We tend to be quite critical" of ourselves. (This study was confined to women. Ginis suspects men might have similar reactions, but less strong because they tend to be less self-critical than women. But that's another story.)[3]

For health clubs, the solution may be simple: provide "mirror-free zones." But the situation is more complex in offices. Just because the walls have nothing but the occasional employee-of-the-month plaque doesn't mean that mirrors aren't everywhere. We just can't see them. We all have an invisible mirror in what Shakespeare called our mind's eye. Throughout the day, our performance is reflected in our mental mirror. Who monitors that reflection? Our very own, internal critic. So the more we focus on the mirror, the more flaws we are likely to find . . . and the more demotivated we may become.

"The Good Soldier"

> "Why is it," queried the leader at a services company, "that we believe our operations are on solid ground one day, and then the very next we find ourselves in mid-air falling straight over the cliff?"

Customer satisfaction measures for the eight call centers were jumping up and down like kids on a trampoline. Over the course of a month, target performance levels would be exceeded for several days running and then drop precipitously. Apparently for no good reason. Same people, same technology, same customers.

The overlooked answer: the leaders were not listening to key middle managers, and they kept piling on accountabilities. Call center managers were expected to handle day-to-day operations, help sell new prospects, launch service enhancements, and integrate new clients. Wanting to be good soldiers, they weren't objecting. But their fragmented jobs caused too many rushed hallway conversations, resulting in distracted responses and a growing list of missed deadlines or service failures.

The heart of the problem was in the minds of the middle managers; they were afraid that bringing up genuine concerns would reflect poorly on them. They wouldn't be seen as team players; they would be judged to be weak, lazy, or unworthy. So they kept quiet. *Looking* good had become more important than *being* good.

Once senior leaders became aware of the pattern, they became better attuned to the early warning signals of an impending blow up. More important, the middle managers were encouraged to push back against unreasonable deadlines. The result: collaboration on smarter ways to balance work assignments led to consistent performance on customer satisfaction metrics.

The more we obsess (even unconsciously) about our unseen audience, the more we are distracted by watching ourselves in our internal mirror, the less energy we have to deal with the real challenges of the present moment. A flurry of thoughts—assumptions about what other people expect, imagining what they're thinking about us, judgment against our own expectations of what we should do or be—crowds out insight and wisdom. We cut ourselves off from the flow of fresh perspective that is available when our minds are clear.

Such habits of performativity first become ingrained during our years in school. Rewards accrue when we are able to absorb information and repeat it to the satisfaction of the teachers filling out our report cards. Sadly, we buy intellectual approval at the expense of genuine intelligence.

Consider, for example, students of global business participating in Phoenix University online classes taught by Ignacio. His final exam requires analysis of a case study in light of several complex questions. "There are always many ways to look at a business problem," Ignacio repeatedly reminds his class. "I want to see how you think." And yet, all too often the students strain to come up with the one *right* answer. That's the outcome of years spent in performativity mode.

Performativity: The Well-Meaning Saboteur

Conventional: Protect the Ego	Step Up: Pursue the Possible

When the boss gives an assignment:

There are no questions	It's easy to ask for clarification
It's hard to try something new	It's easy to act like a beginner
It's hard to say "I don't know"	It's easy to admit limits

When a problem/issue is being discussed:

Conversation is a rapid-fire volley	Space between sentences allows reflection
Interruptions abound; people finish others' sentences (often incorrectly)	Each person listens to the others

When someone disagrees, the reaction is:

Defensiveness	Inquiry
"They must think I'm stupid"	"How interesting that we see things differently"

Indeed, countless entry-level professionals grapple with performativity as they make the transition from school to work. You assign a task to an eager young person. She dives into it with full enthusiasm, putting in loads of overtime. At the deadline, she delivers a long, intricate, highly polished product . . . that just happens to be off base.

What's going wrong?

As a good manager, you look at the total responsibility of your team. You assign to your eager young employee a fair share of that responsibility—appropriate to her talent, ability, and experience. You see her work as a piece of a puzzle.

She, however, still in the thrall of academe, sees homework: an assignment designed to prove her mettle. She assumes that you expect her to do this on her own, ultimately to turn in a finished product that will earn a good grade. She doesn't feel she has permission to ask for clarification or help, or to get feedback on preliminary ideas in a give-and-take process. It seems natural to her that the performativity she mastered at school will serve her well in the office.

The Power in Calm

Why is it important to break the unseen mirror? Because performativity restricts our natural ability to access regenerative resources. Our ego interferes with our natural wisdom. We are so obsessed with self-image that we don't see available choices. We cut off our connection to the best parts of ourselves, and to others.

This plays out almost every day on the popular court programs—such as *Judge Judy*. In a typical case, the plaintiff complained that the defendant had hit him. But the defendant pleaded self-defense: the plaintiff had yelled and made gestures; so the defendant stopped his car, got out, and punched the plaintiff. "You were driving away," noted the judge. "How could you feel you needed to defend yourself?" Replied the defendant: "Because he yelled at me." Nothing physical had happened, but the defendant did not—could not—distinguish between his *thought* about the plaintiff's challenge and real, physical violence.

In other words, when we are worried, distracted, busy, or just trying too hard, it is difficult to be patient enough for common sense to emerge. Our noisy mind obscures the natural resource that can make it easier to produce good work: the soft voice of insight. The very nature of insight, literally "sight from within," means that answers don't necessarily come from acquired knowledge. Working harder doesn't produce insight. Rather, it is a revelation that emerges from our wisdom or common sense only when our thinking is tranquil. Truly productive breakthroughs—those ah-HA! moments—often come to mind when we may not be thinking of anything in particular.

High-Wire Productivity

Conventional: Try Harder	Step Up: Less Produces More
Plug in 24/7, via technology	Set aside time to recharge mental batteries
React to the urgent	Focus on what is most important
Find complications	Sift out the essential steps
"Ready, fire, aim"	Allow the outcomes to guide actions
"No pain, no gain"	Graceful, "no sweat" progress
Not enough hours in the day	Time seems to slow down

Reactive Mode: Who's at the Wheel?

Unfortunately, most of us spend very little time making distinctions about the quality of our thinking. Too often we react to external prods before engaging our internal game: stopping to consider what action *should* be taken.

An e-mail arrives; irritated, we fire off our reply, generating an electronic cascade across the organization, no matter how unworthy the topic. We respond curtly to a voice mail without bothering to consider the effect on the recipient—will we inadvertently send him into a tailspin for the rest of the day? Or we make an off-hand comment during someone's presentation that is interpreted as a definitive judgment about the proposal under discussion; a ten-cent question (maybe the boss is just musing out loud) may generate thousands of dollars of busywork chasing down the answer. Sometimes the simplest issue spins out of control as one person after another reacts.

Reflective Thinking: The More Productive Mode

Any manager can get off track, just as any company can trend downhill. What is reassuring, to us and to our teams, is the knowledge that when our thinking is clear, answers will emerge. There is a self-correcting, innate mechanism we can rely on to regain our bearings: *Reflective Thinking.*

Our minds are wonderful instruments, useful for many kinds of tasks. One mode of thinking is logical, or analytical, reasoning. It has valuable application for such things as figuring out a numerical problem, planning a trip, making a list. Engineers and other scientists revel in being able to use this faculty to solve problems in the physical world. Most issues in business already have a good procedure known to work, and logic often suffices to get the job done.

But people who think solely with this method may sometimes find themselves out of synch with others. Perhaps it's because this form of thinking is so absorbing that people lose sight of the big picture—they get caught up in the fine points. That might be okay if your job is primarily about performing detailed tasks.

However, when the issue is novel or when something is not working well, reflective thinking yields a better result. In that mode, the manager steps back from the nitty-gritty, seeks a calm mental state, asks himself a question, and then sees what fresh thought comes to mind.

Reflective Thinking and Resiliency

Max was preparing an important presentation that would ask senior executives to approve a completely new concept for the company, a virtual contact center to be stitched together from three call centers currently reporting to different organizations. Six months of hard work could easily be undone, depending on the dynamics of the upcoming meeting. And the business leaders involved didn't always get along.

Typically, Max would be stressed out. But he'd learned about reflective thinking. So, while preparing as thoroughly as he always did, he consciously avoided succumbing to worried thoughts. As the meeting began, he maintained a bit of emotional distance, staying interested in how the executives would reach a decision rather than counting on a specific outcome.

Within the first two minutes, one of the executives interrupted Max's presentation, questioning the commitment of the call center managers to the new concept. Instead of reacting defensively, Max really listened to what the executive was saying. He realized that she had an excellent question. So he abandoned his script and stopped the proceedings. He quickly rounded up the three managers, brought them into the room, and had *them* answer the question. Case closed.

Mike would never have done this in the past, considering it way too risky; after all, the managers had not been prepped. This time, his calm, aware mental state made it easy to absorb feedback and adjust— and to depend on his colleagues to rise to the occasion.

"What a different experience!" he said later. "And it seemed so obvious and natural. I would never have been able to adjust like that before I saw how the quality of my thinking affects my experience. It's a whole new reality!"

How Busy Managers Derail Progress

It's not what the manager *says* that affects productivity; it's what he *does*. For example, Bob used to worry a lot. In fact, he assumed that worry was a good thing. Worry was a friend that helped him pay attention to details, to adequately prepare for the future, to ensure that he covered all the bases. Bob even worried about not worrying enough.

As the people who reported to him picked up his habit of thinking, they began to find their own "good reasons" to worry. Teamwide productivity dropped. Countless person-hours were wasted ruminating about outcomes that never came to be, or anticipating the worst in the midst of success.

Meanwhile, as a habitual second-guesser, Betsy would take a quick look at a problem and make a few bold strokes to tackle it. In short order, however, she'd rehash the decision, often requiring follow-up conversations and re-dos. And then she'd wonder why the people who reported to her seemed to hang back, why nothing would get done unless she finished it herself.

But, as we have seen, we have a choice of whether to entertain these and other negative habits. Instead, we can look toward what seems intriguing, interesting, or inspiring. That turn of mind evokes constructive feelings, which can then guide productive behavior.

Too Simple to Be Believed?

Unproductive thinking habits are so deeply ingrained that we usually can't see them. Recognizing the futility of such wheel-spinning, our impulse is to learn self-help techniques.

But techniques that add one more layer of effort, one more set of demands that require mental energy, are ultimately doomed to fail.

The high-wire approach to productivity may seem too easy to believe. But over and over, we've seen positive results. As we pay less attention to external pressures and the emotional reactions that they engender and more attention to the quality of our thinking, extraneous effort vanishes.

How do you stop to reflect instead of react? Just hit the mental pause button. Notice whatever emotion arises, but choose not to act on it. Stop, even for a moment. Take a drink of water. Get up from your desk. Stretch. Ask yourself a question—"What's truly important about what I just heard or saw?" Create, in other words, a mental break so that you may connect to your Mother Wit.

As a matter of fact, you already know techniques to achieve the state we're describing. You may work out, jog, walk, swim; draw or paint, knit or sew; listen to music or play an instrument; practice yoga and/or deep breathing; play with your children or pets; spend time at the beach or in the woods; meditate, even pray. Far from taking time away from what's really important, such mental breaks are an investment in greater productivity. Even a few minutes "away" can leave you refreshed, renewed, reenergized—and closer to a solution.

As we give free rein to a sense of well-being, our mood lightens and our minds grow calm. Our energy and intelligence are applied to achieving progress, rather than brooding over the way external pressures might over-whelm our ability to respond. The most onerous task becomes easier to ac-complish when our feelings about it are positive or even neutral—"this is just something that comes with the job"—instead of negative.

High-Wire Key to Averting Burnout While Achieving Results: Don't Try So Hard

In short, there's a fundamental difference between being busy and being productive. The path we take is a function not of the work itself, but what's inside our heads. How much needless work we and our teams can innocently add to the simplest task simply by not thinking clearly! We get caught up in a cycle of anxiety and busyness when we don't sort out what's important from what isn't, what I need to do versus what I can delegate, or the net benefit/loss of undertaking a task versus ignoring it.

Ironically, the greatest hindrance to productivity is not daydreaming or idleness, but the idea that our natural process of regeneration has no place at work. Productive people understand, perhaps instinctively, that an affirmative and steady state of mind is our most helpful resource. They gain productivity not by a learned technique, but by thinking differently.

Start making the change at once by beginning to ask yourself and others the kind of questions that help sort out what's urgent from what's important:

"What are we *really* trying to accomplish?"

"Am I sure there isn't a different way around obstacles?"

"Am I or are others reacting with intense emotion that could cloud our judgment?"

"Most important, am I in the right frame of mind—calm, clear, confident—to tackle this?"

So if you want to be more productive, don't try harder—working all night or setting an earlier wake-up call. Instead, harness the energy being wasted in anxiety or performativity. Staying calm, focused, and curious leads us to do what is essential—no more, no less. Genuine productivity is the result: far more valuable outputs with far less input.

> The butterfly counts
> not months but moments,
> and has time enough.
>
> —Rabidranath Tagore,
> Indian writer/philosopher

CHAPTER 3

Creativity and Strategy

Key question: Creativity and strategic thinking seem to belong to an anointed few. Can I find those talents in myself?

The operating management of a pharmaceutical company was stymied. They'd been meeting for hours, but couldn't get past a logjam: trying to decide which to do first—get on with the detailed planning of their cost reduction program, or spend more time clarifying vision and purpose so that the organization had context for the belt-tightening that was soon to come. Unable to resolve the dilemma, they put the question aside and broke for the day.

The next morning they found that, independently, about half the group had arrived at the same thought—namely, to work in a context broad enough for *both* imperatives: Integrate the contextual reasons directly into each project so that the reasons for making change were crystal clear. The impasse of the day before melted away. Follow-on steps seemed obvious, and decisions clicked into place.

We all have had the experience of trying to force an answer by will power, looking to solve a problem using just our intellect. We're familiar with the bleak feelings that characterize this mode—anxiety, pressure, muddle, frustration.

It doesn't have to be that way. We can, instead, do as the above group did: rely on a powerful tool available to each of us, our mental "back burner."

It's easy to lose sight of the fact that the thinking that we direct consciously is but a small percentage of what our minds are actually doing in every moment. With a little bit of gentle programming, we can put our unconscious powers to work on pending decisions. It's a simple process: drop the effort of trying to solve a problem; turn down the mental heat, so to speak, and put the issue on the back burner. You're not being irresponsible. Quite the contrary. The topic remains active under the surface—like the swan who looks graceful from the neck up, but whose feet are paddling furiously underwater. While you're walking around the office, driving home, eating dinner, even sleeping, your mind continues to sift and sort. You might wake up with a sudden solution, or find a fresh perspective as soon as you turn your attention back to the problem. And did you ever notice how smart you seem when you are taking a shower or traveling on vacation?

That's the value of your back burner. Obvious solutions emerge for the most intractable problems, and new ideas pop up. Such answers are coming from a source of understanding that goes beyond acquired knowledge—from what we sometimes refer to as Mother Wit, also called common sense, wisdom, intuition, or gut instinct.

The back burner is one of the secrets used by productive people. It's a key element behind the truism: "If you want something done, then give it to the busiest person." Paradoxically, to do more, they think less—or, at least, with less conscious effort. In truth, we can *all* access this inborn resource (call it our unconscious wisdom) anytime, anywhere—provided we keep our thinking even-paced instead of giving in to fear, uncertainty, self-criticism, and their ilk. The common denominator in both creativity and strategy is the capacity of every thinker to find a fresh solution by trusting the mental power that lies just beneath memories, experiences, or acquired knowledge. And that puts the lie to the conventional belief that creativity and strategy are provinces of a special few.

How Do They *Do* That?

Bob once lent his summer home to an artist. When his family returned, they found that their tenant had twisted a rusted anchor wire around some driftwood, sculpting a graceful ballerina. It still stands next to their front porch.

Most of us wonder: how did the artist do that? Certain individuals seem special, able to express themselves inventively, regardless of their circumstances. You find them in every organization—usually anointed with a title or job description that gives them exclusive rights to handle assignments that require creativity. But they seem to be rare talents. Most of us assume that our default process is to think "inside the box."

Rubbish.

Creativity is simply insight put into action.

Creativity, in fact, is innate in and available to every human being. Every child can put a crayon to a page and then earnestly describe animals and people that look like mere scribbles to the adult. As we grow to adulthood and go into business, we put away childish things; we shut off "frivolous imaginings." We are encouraged to assume the roles our parents have scripted for us, to satisfy the expectations of our teachers, to take the opinions of others seriously, to bow to the fashions of our contemporaries. In short, we stop playing and go to work. As if the two were necessarily incompatible.

Somehow, a few individuals resist confinement and allow their thinking to meander. How? Simply by keeping open a channel to the creative force that is all around, and in, all of us.

High-Wire Creativity

Conventional: Special Talent	Step Up: Universal Resource
Anoint the few	Expect the unexpected from the entire team
Indulging talent	Channeling insight
"Childish"	"Childlike"
Call on creativity occasionally	Hang out in the unknown
Tension between creativity and "the norm"	No need for limits

Perhaps many of us close that channel because it's not always comfortable. Creation is dynamic; it tears apart neatly drawn maps. Mountains bear silent witness to this fact. Once the land was flat; on the surface, all seemed still. Yet underneath, tectonic forces were at work. Tension built until titanic collisions thrust peaks upward toward the sky.

In business, things go along smoothly until the "what ifs" begin to jab and stab at the confining edges of the box, the limits of the known. In creating the new we, too, may be required to tear apart the old. That may seem terrifying. But as we saw in chapter 1, each of us has been given unseen gifts to help us embrace the future. And to put our creativity to work.

Thinking Strategically

Like creativity, strategic thinking uses the inborn ingenuity available to all of us. If it seems that some people access those resources more easily than others, it's just that they are demonstrating nimbleness—a mental flexibility or awareness—that illuminates what is truly important.

And what is truly important in business? The central choices facing all organizations are: "What is possible, given what matters to us?" and "What goals do we wish to achieve, given what is possible?" The first describes the company's vision; the second sets forth its purpose, the goals that seem relevant. These questions are fundamental for teams, departments, divisions, and organizations as a whole. They inspire people by enlisting them in a purpose that gives meaning to their work life.

Strategy answers the follow-on choices: "*How* do we attain our goals?" Strategies without goals are little more than dogs chasing their tails. But goals without strategy are little more than empty dreams. Ultimately, strategy shapes *doing*.

Those who rely solely on research and analysis develop plans that seem sound—at least on paper. But however sensible it seems, the purely logical approach tends to be a dry, mechanical, lifeless process. It generates documents that may never be referred to again instead of enthusiasm for the journey ahead. And it takes too long, becoming in many companies a never ending cycle.

So, all too often, people bumble along, making decisions and taking actions without a robust understanding of what is truly important. Or they wait to be told what to do, or to receive feedback about whether or not they are doing the right thing. In the inevitable confusion, it is difficult to harness the organization's resources, and opportunities are often missed. By the time the barn door has been secured, the horse is long gone.

There is another way—the continuous process of directing the collective intelligence to the question, "How do we make progress toward our goal *today*?"

High-Wire Strategy

Conventional: Roadmap to Goals	Step Up: Rigor in Choice
Research + analysis	Reflection + research + analysis + reflection
Arduous process	Fast-paced and invigorating
Scheduled	Happens continuously
Channeled through formulas	Develops organically
Seeking *the* answer	"There's always another way"
Takes a long time; may miss opportunities	As fast as insight; nimbly responsive
Formalized document	Continual invention and refinement

Stretching the Bonds of Time

"Acting strategically" happens in companies that see strategy as a continual process of invention and refinement: *invention* in the sense of creating novel solutions that propel the organization toward its goals, *refinement* in the sense of building expertise that makes possible ever-greater accomplishment. In this process, the definition of "now" becomes elastic. Almost any task can take on new meaning when it is understood as part of something larger. Seeing a small step within a broad perspective creates a clear sense of its importance and actually illuminates something that lies in the distance. Thus, in a sense strategy stretches the bonds of time in a way that motivates action.

Such companies as Dow Chemical, General Electric, and Bank of America come to mind. Each has been constant in its purpose (Bank of America kept a single set of goals for 20 years!), but flexible in its methods (GE has deployed multiple programs—Six Sigma to Workout—over the past ten years). And they are not afraid to set goals even when they have no idea how they will achieve them (Dow's leaders committed in 1995 to reducing costs so that the company could achieve a positive return on economic capital at the bottom of a recession).

In studying such companies, we may see the steps that led to success, but fail to understand the deeper principles at work. Great strategy is always obvious. What may be subtle is what a leader does to elicit it. Our experience has taught us that the greatest results stem from what we call "Reflective Strategy" (figure 3.1)

How do we stimulate such thinking in ourselves, and in others? First, we rely on the fact that everyone has inner resources of common sense. Next, we are not afraid to keep exploring the most relevant questions. Key strategic questions are straightforward, seemingly simple:

"How do we achieve progress today?"

"What needs to happen after that?"

"When do we need to have reached this milestone?"

"Who is best positioned and most passionate about driving the action?"

Staying in these questions, being comfortable "not knowing the answer," stimulates our teams to reflect more deeply and, thus, to generate powerful ideas or insights. When someone brings up the past or imagines the future from an insecure stance, thoughts of negative possibilities seem like foregone conclusions; they appear *real* to him. The wise manager knows to listen carefully to whatever someone is saying, maintaining a positive flow by asking questions from a stance of sincere interest. In as little as a moment or two, even

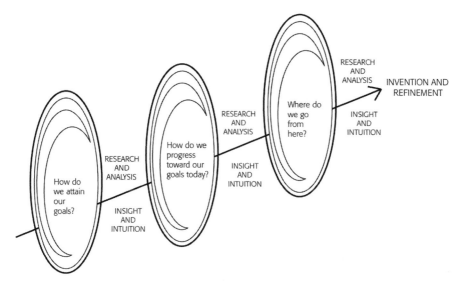

FIGURE 3.1

Goals are, by their very nature, future-oriented. But because we live day to day, it may be hard for us to see beyond current obstacles or to understand how to translate a future aspiration into practical action now. "Reflective strategy" is a way of thinking that extends our understanding of "now" to embrace the future with a perspective unfettered by fears and anxieties about what could go wrong. We are, in a sense, stretching the boundaries of time.

the most confused or insecure person may be able to see that his anxieties originated and exist only in his thoughts.

One of our clients once praised the strategic thinking of a team member. We found this puzzling because we couldn't recall a single suggestion or piece of advice that person had delivered. But the client said: "She asks great questions; she gets me to think about things I hadn't considered before."

Delighted to Be Wrong

Mac was sure there was no solution to the problem faced by the U.S. Potato Board: the low-carb diet craze had a lock on consumers, and there was nothing the potato industry could say to change those attitudes. A talented marketing veteran, Mac had looked at every possible angle, played with multiple messages. Nothing would work.

So he was skeptical when a consulting firm was brought in, but he was willing to join the team exploring communications strategy. They started with what they knew about potatoes and what they thought they knew about their customers. But then they actually watched a focus group and found that consumers heard things differently than the marketers had assumed. For example, because interest in nutrition had soared, the marketers assumed that consumers would know that potatoes have a high content of potassium. But that fact not only surprised the focus group participants, it got them interested in reconsidering their decisions about what to eat.

Based on what they heard, the marketers crafted possible messages, favorably comparing potatoes to bananas as a source of potassium. They showed those to a second group—whose reaction again took them by surprise; they were too skeptical to accept a simple statement of facts. Those findings led to yet another set of possible messages. This time a new focus group was shown an actual label approved by the FDA; instantly, they were convinced.

The reiterative process of crafting-and-checking messages led to new realizations about what could be said in a way that would make a difference. From that focal point, the board created its most successful communications program in 15 years—a burst of ads and newspaper articles centered on the FDA-approved label. All because Mac and his colleagues had the courage and commitment to challenge beliefs about which they were *absolutely sure*.

The Creatively Strategic/Strategically Creative Process

Both creativity and strategy must transcend analysis and memory. If the solution were in what we already know, wouldn't we have done it by now?

Of course, we need to gather all relevant facts and gain a thorough understanding of our goal, our situation, and the obstacles we must overcome. But at some point we must stop actively crunching data and combing existing information and let insight happen. While no technique exists to call up insight on demand, we can take steps that establish a favorable environment—one that stimulates fresh thinking.

How can we know when we are close to an insight? By a kind of mental tickle that demands to be scratched—often experienced as a feeling of surprise, puzzlement, or paradox.

Surprise is the unexpected: based on everything that we already know, we project what is likely to happen. If B has followed A, can C be far behind? But if 6 suddenly shows up, that triggers surprise. For example, in the three months following the terrorist attacks on the World Trade Center and the Pentagon, cooking school enrollments soared. Initially surprising, that simple fact opened a stream of speculation about the marketing fallout from America's rekindled appreciation for togetherness, a yearning to feel cozy and cared for in a warm kitchen at home.

Stimulating Strategy and Creativity

Nobody does her best thinking when she is anxious. Managers create an environment that encourages insight by modeling openness. You don't need to *do* something that adds steps to the process; in fact, you can actually save time by changing the *way you are.*

Rather than trying to control idea sessions, take such steps as:

- Ask simple questions, especially if jargon is involved. Does everyone ascribe the same meaning to the terms being used?
- Pay attention to how you're feeling. Does something you hear or see trigger a familiar feeling—perhaps you've encountered a similar situation before; what worked then? Or does it generate uneasiness— perhaps indicating a disconnect with your values?
- Step back from the immediate issue. What's the bigger context, the broader perspective?
- Consider the whole as you study a part; understand the part in relation to the whole (similar to the process chosen by the pharmaceutical company at the start of this chapter).
- Look for parallels, analogies, even metaphors in nonrelated fields. What have you learned in other parts of your life—sports, hobbies, family—that might apply?
- Ultimately: enjoy exploring.[1]

Puzzlement occurs when we encounter something that couldn't possibly be true, but is. It just doesn't fit the familiar. For example, a few years ago researchers asked teenaged boys what they would do if they had a million dollars. A normal assumption would have been, "buy a car." Instead, the most frequent response was, "save it." That puzzling fact led a marketing strategist to look further. She noticed that a high percentage of those boys, unlike teens in her generation, knew someone who had been fired or laid off. And that generated a different sense of teenagers' concerns.

A *paradox* appears to be self-contradictory: opposites seem to occupy the same space. A growing percentage of Americans say that it's bad to be overweight and that they're on a diet, yet sales of dessert items continue to rise. That paradox provides important direction to food marketers.

Whenever you find yourself dealing with surprise, puzzlement, or paradox, take note. These are valuable signposts. There's an insight up ahead that can point the way to being creatively strategic.

When Organizations Get Stuck

The power of this approach recently became apparent to Bruce, head of the quality function at a health-care firm. He had brought his direct reports together to brainstorm how they could be more influential with plant managers and the manufacturing VPs. So often, those operating managers would ignore quality issues until a small event became a big problem.

Bruce's team had been working all afternoon and was getting cranky. "Come on, guys," Bruce exhorted. "We need some good ideas here. I don't understand why you people can see the problem clearly, but don't have any relevant suggestions about what we ought to do. Am I supposed to come up with all the answers?" Silence ensued. The mood turned palpably sour. The facilitator called for a five-minute break and walked Bruce down the hall.

"What are you feeling, Bruce?" the facilitator asked.

"Frustrated!" he replied. "I know my staff has some great ideas, and I was hoping that we could really use the next two hours to finish this brainstorm and then put the ideas into action right away. But they sure don't want to play today."

"I see it a bit differently," said the outsider. "It's already been a long day, and they are tired; not the best frame of mind to do the kind of creatively strategic work you are asking them to accomplish. Why don't you take a step back and see what comes to mind."

By the time Bruce walked back into the room, he was able to make a shift. "Guys, I am sorry," he began. "I think that I have been pushing us too hard today, and we may all be a bit too tired to pursue this tough issue. We need to be at our best mentally, and I sure don't feel that way myself."

One of the managers, Steve, spoke up: "Boy, am I glad you said that! Just before you called for the break, I was watching the clock like I was in the last period back in high school."

Everyone laughed. No one spoke for a minute or two. Another manager broke the silence: "Perhaps we could take five minutes and go around the table asking ourselves, 'what is the single most important operational impact we could have?' "

"That's a good idea," offered Steve. "I think I can do that if we then promise to adjourn and not discuss implementation until we have dinner."

Quickly, each person put his or her most obvious suggestion on the table. Bruce had to remind them just once that no discussion would be allowed right then. Within 15 minutes, he had a comprehensive list of ideas. Later, over dinner, the group spontaneously came to consensus: one suggestion stood out above all the rest. Bruce then guided them in a 45-minute exploration of how best to put that idea into practice.

By noon the next day, two members of the team had already engaged their staff in starting to make changes happen. Bruce was ecstatic. He had experienced the benefits of the creatively strategic (or strategically creative) three-step:

- Get the participants in the right frame of mind: easy, relaxed, but attentive
- Put just one question to them
- Let them run with the ball

Bruce's brainstorm experience points to the important question: Given that everyone has the source of creative and strategic thinking within her, why do organizations continually get stuck? Because their leaders try to force answers, instead of giving fresh ideas enough space to emerge.

To nurture creativity and strategy, managers participate in a kind of mental relay race. Start down the track to resolve a tough issue or make a bold decision, sifting through data and facts for as long as you're able to do so with ease. As soon as you find that you're going over and over the same loops of thought, stop. Instead of pushing mental abilities to the limit, exerting more and more pressure, rest your mind. Clear the thought filters that block access to the deeper reservoirs of your intelligence. Mentally, "pass the baton" to your subconscious; pick up other matters, attend to other business, or just take a break. Once the debris flushes out from your intellectual filters, what start flowing through your mental pipes are common sense, perspective, and insight. When you feel their energy, run another mental lap—until you again feel stuck. Then again engage your back burner—repeating the process as many times as necessary to achieve ultimate resolution.

This may appear lackadaisical to some. They may question why you are not pulling and pushing aggressively on Topic A. Too many traditional bosses pay more attention to the employee who has been working so hard that she melts down in the hallway than to the quiet performer getting things done without a lot of drama. But our experience—in our own businesses and consulting with countless organizations—is that relying on the back burner actually allows us to make faster progress. We use intuition to leap ahead quickly, or use common sense to see more straightforward ways to implement decisions.

High-Wire Key to Fostering Creativity and Strategy: Institutionalize Curiosity

The strategically creative/creatively strategic process begins with asking the right questions. And what are those questions? There's no all-purpose list that you can memorize. Rather, the appropriate probes will occur to you as you listen in the moment. But the right *kind* of questions will be those that open mental doors and windows.

The old standbys—why, what, how, when, who, even where—are the ones to use. Begin with the "why"; allow people to engage, sense when they begin to come to a natural close, test to see if there is agreement or understanding, then turn to the next most obvious issue. Be careful not to distract by asking questions too quickly. Allow time to process one stream of thinking at a time. And don't shift gears and ask something that points in an entirely new direction until the preceding question is resolved.

In short, ask questions that encourage openness rather than argument. Ask neutral questions that unblock the flow of thinking. Approach each new problem with an unencumbered thought process. Drop all assumptions, all preconceptions. Be open to possibility. That's the key to unlocking the universal capacity for creativity and strategic thinking.

> What you are living is but a fractional inkling of what is really within you, what gives you life, breadth, and depth.
>
> —Joseph Campbell, *The Power of Myth*

CHAPTER 4

Better Decisions

Key question: How can I make sound decisions, the kind that inspire confident action by my team?

Something just didn't feel right to the leader of an accounts payable team at one of the world's largest computer manufacturers. As she was walking home from work one day, she thought about an apparent increase in the number of new leasing vendors as well as in the dollars charged by existing suppliers. She wondered if her team members had noticed anything unusual and made a mental note to bring up the matter at the next weekly meeting.

No one recalled seeing anything out of the ordinary. So this manager could have just dropped the issue. Instead, she asked the team to track invoices for the next week. Once people started to look in this direction, they saw a pattern of unusual activity. In fact, payments were three times higher than normal.

The manager realized that she needed to learn more. She asked other accounts payable teams to check their data. She learned that a recently issued corporate directive called for limits on capital expenditures. The picture suddenly came into focus: throughout the company, people were rushing to lease equipment before the new policy went into effect—complying with the letter, but not the spirit, of the directive.

Still this manager resisted taking action. First, she asked the question, "What is the best course, given what I know?" Three or four options came to mind. She chose the one that seemed most obvious: to present her findings to her director and to the head of shared services. The corporate controller was immediately brought into the conversation. Within 20 minutes, the four determined a series of actions to control this spending.

A serious situation was addressed and resolved simply and directly. All because a team leader had an insight, took the time to reflect on it, explored the situation from a stance of inquisitiveness, and then involved others to determine the best path forward. Unfortunately, it's often not this easy. How many times have you witnessed or been party to a flawed decision or wrongheaded action? Or perhaps wondered why no one stepped forward to make an obvious choice when the need for action was apparent to all?

These patterns have a common denominator: they happen when people are too wrapped up in personal thinking to see the big picture. We lose connection with the larger purpose or fail to gain perspective about the opportunity at hand. It's a case of getting wrapped around the axle of egocentric thoughts and not realizing it. Despite our best intentions, we are caught in an intellectual game that makes it impossible to tap our inborn wisdom. So decisions come hard.

Instead, inspiring managers facilitate an ongoing, exploratory process that makes sure the right questions are addressed and, even more important, that the hidden resources of the organization are tapped. As we saw in chapter 3, this often becomes a step-by-step cycle of:

- Reflection and discovery, leading to . . .
- Action and results, leading to . . .
- Further reflection, leading to revised action and even better results.

High-Wire Planning

Conventional: Analyzing	Step Up: Innovating
Research past successes	Reflect on the right issue
Accept an expert's answer	Challenge assumptions
Look for quick resolution	Hang out in the question
Try to copy someone else's answer (e.g., competitors)	Rely on the ingenuity of the team

I Don't Know

The first step toward reflective decision making is to open to the collective wisdom of the team. To put it simply: the effort of any one person, no matter how talented, is dwarfed by the contributions of many. This is so obvious that it needs no proof. But putting that belief into action requires a willingness to acknowledge that possibilities exist beyond our own knowledge or experience.

In other words, the counterintuitive secret of managers who make decisions that rally the troops is an unshakable security and comfort in saying three little words: I. Don't. Know.

"I don't know." These three words relieve us of the burden of analyzing or processing, of feeling frustrated or impatient, of struggling to remember a technique or a formula for success. These words can galvanize staff, for they imply a faith in the team's ability that encourages engagement.

It may feel hard to say, "I don't know." It takes humility or, at least, a temporary setting aside of ego. But it opens the door to learning and to understanding. These three words liberate us from being stuck in any sort of rut; they set us on an adventure of discovering something fresh.

Instead of indicating an unacceptable weakness, "I don't know" means simply: "Nothing occurs to me at the moment. The answer isn't in my experience or learning, but I expect that an insight will come to me—*or to someone else on our team.*"

Innovation flourishes only when people are not afraid to explore a question, to look away from what they already know, to distrust assumptions (such as, "we have always done things this way" or "that won't work")—as Mac and the Potato Board learned in the example cited in chapter 3. This goes against our training; we've been taught since elementary school that it's important to know *the* answer. And it goes against our beliefs about work. After all, weren't we hired or promoted because someone thought we already had the required knowledge and skill for the position?

True, when the boss asks a question, we're apt to feel a twinge of fear. We've been in meetings where the boss has blown up because he couldn't get the information he thought he needed. Our automatic assumption is that we're being tested, not consulted. Suddenly, our very job seems to be at risk. Yet aren't we putting ourselves under unnecessary pressure with unrealistic expectations? How can we anticipate every question that might be asked?

Thought Habits That Impede Good Decisions

Ego: "It has always been important for me to look good"—so that we cannot see what action is best for the whole team

Greed: "What's in it for me?"—so that we throw obstacles in the path of others' progress

Fear: "You think this is bad? Well, let me tell you how bad things could get!"—to the point that everyone is afraid to act

A Word about Ethics

Robert Caro, Lyndon B. Johnson's biographer, was asked during an interview by National Public Radio, "Must power corrupt?" As a writer who has spent his whole life studying powerful people, his answer was, "No, power *reveals*." Reveals the person's deeply rooted character for all to see.

What do others see in you?

When a manager's deed points to the greater good, we say that he exhibits good character. But behavior happens in real time. It is not like we can retreat back to our office, indulge in a leisurely process to decide the action most consistent with good character, and then put it into practice. Nope. Managing happens in the moment. A choice is made in the blink of an eye.

Sharp is the razor's edge for the manager—the smallest slip may cause a free fall. Even if he seems to get away with something, a manager has actually placed his foot on thin air when he finds justification for pushing someone to back-date a document, encouraging the reversal of a bad-debt write-off, or asking a question that gives the tacit go-ahead for creating a sham transaction. As one of the jurors who convicted Martha Stewart in March 2004 told the *Wall Street Journal:* "We all felt terrible about it at the end. It felt like such a foolish mistake that was increased as it went along."

So how does a manager learn to exhibit good character reliably? No matter what the circumstance, no matter how great the pressure to deliver quick returns, how do you trust that you will make the right choice?

Begin by noting the words used to denote "good character"—such as integrity, honesty, respect, fairness, truthfulness. Then contemplate the meaning behind those words. Most important, identify the *feelings* you associate with those words. For example, our colleague Alexander knows that telling the truth helps him feel *"free, as if I am floating, unafraid of my past."* He knows that when these feelings are present, his decisions will guide his behavior to correct deeds.

Perhaps you take shortcuts because "everybody does it." Indeed, the bad news is that the culture, the character of an institution, can only be changed one person at a time. The good news is that you can be that person.

"Overwhelming" is not too strong a description for the task of knowing everything.

We've all seen what happens when leaders are not willing to admit that they don't know it all; truth be told, we've been there, done that, ourselves. We become self-righteous, defending our view ever more loudly, as if volume alone could make something true. To be effective, managers must discover the power of adopting an open perspective, readily asking, "What do *you* think?"

The state of "not knowing" can be strikingly energizing. Even if the deadline is near, the leader's job is to put that out of mind so that she may access her own mental capacity and bring out the best from everyone.

Dare to Decide Differently

Getting started on reflective decision making can be as simple as just remembering to ask a why, what, how, when, who, or where question when confronting an issue or opportunity. Virtually any substantive question will do, *provided* you look to find out what it is you don't know instead of confirming an existing assumption.

Shigeo Shingo's famous "Five Whys" embodies this approach. Shingo was the engineer who worked out solutions to many of the obstacles to the "lean production system," which the Japanese implemented many years ago. The technique is simple. When confronting an opportunity, problem, failure, mistake, or unexpected result, ask the question, "why," five times. Each "why" goes a layer deeper until the root cause becomes apparent. "Five Whys" illustrates how easily we find overlooked factors when we apply our common sense with a touch of analytic elbow grease.

(1) Why was I late to the meeting? I ran out of gas. (2) Why did I run out of gas? I didn't have time to stop at a gas station. (3) Why didn't I have time to stop? I didn't realize how far away the meeting was. (4) Why didn't I realize how far away the meeting was? I didn't check the directions. (5) Why didn't I check the directions? I made an assumption that it was going to be near the boss's office. Maybe if I didn't make assumptions like that, I'd avoid more problems. . . .

Try it yourself. Apply the "Five Whys" to typical business issues, such as:

- Why are we having so much trouble making our numbers?
- Why are we having trouble finding/keeping staff?
- Why are we missing deadlines?

Of course, there is a place for such analytic rigor in making decisions. Knowledge and experience are essential ingredients. Someone who is insightful but not experienced can achieve progress, but he is prone to avoidable mistakes that may cause unnecessary pain.

For example, last summer Bob asked Gavin, a teenaged worker, to remove a pile of old floor joists at his summer residence. Gavin selected a nearby field of weeds as the best place to stack the old joists. It was a creative solution to an eyesore: the weeds would grow to cover the unsightly pile in a matter of days. But a few weeks later, two 12-year-old boys badly cut their shins on the nails sticking out of the wood. Without the experience to anticipate how kids play—always running, taking the most direct route between two points— Gavin had picked a spot on the direct line between the back doors of two cottages.

Ambidextrous Thinking

A big boost to effective management is awareness of the mode in which our mind is operating at any given moment—analysis or insight, logical or reflective—and consideration of whether it is appropriate for the task at hand. Like an athlete who can bat left- or right-handed, we can use the thought process most appropriate to respond to the pitches we will be receiving.

Analysis can help frame the question or evaluate the efficacy of results. But none of us can expect to arrive at optimal decisions solely by mulling over the past or comparing anticipated scenarios. As we've seen, we must reflect on the right questions, exploring the important variables in search of something original.

> Despite conventional wisdom, and the pressures we sometimes put on ourselves in the moment, *leading* is not always synonymous with *doing.*

Reflection in Motion

Toyota has been using this reflective technique for more than 50 years in its efforts to "find a better way." When something is off kilter, they don't jump into a flurry of action, find the culprit, or look to shift the blame. They stop and reflect. The company says that institutional curiosity has been one key to enormous improvement in productivity.[1]

Note that an important part of this process is resisting the urge to run with the first thought; instead, step back and reflect some more. This defies normal operating assumptions, which encourage us to focus on quick fixes, or expect us to have all the answers at our fingertips. Fear of being seen as not doing the job quickly can provoke reflexive behavior. Rising to urgent thoughts, a manager may jump to hasty conclusions that prompt ill-considered action.

But skilled managers are willing to wait for the emergent answer, the fresh thought that can lead to real breakthroughs. They know that only by *reaching beneath the surface* of accumulated experience and knowledge do they find perspective and understanding. Whatever the timeframe, they know that the stronger the link between insights and actions, the better the outcomes. Too often we throw ourselves at a problem or issue, frantically trying to find the solution. We fuss for hours, exhausting ourselves to no avail—or we force action.

Reflection can take as little as a moment. Stop. Take a breath. Disengage. Then ask yourself: what is really going on; what do we need to do? Don't think about it actively; wait to see what pops up. Just as when you're trying to remember something—what was the name of the actor in that movie I saw last month—you drop the effort of remembering, and all at once the answer is *there*. To those hooked on Internet speed, reflective decision making may seem too passive. And having been accustomed to getting things done, your first impulse after promotion may be to move fast to make your mark.

But reflective decision making pays off. First, it reduces risk by making it easier to catch mistakes quickly, when they are small enough to be corrected with minimal effort and cost. Even more important, it facilitates team commitment to the goal because it invites each member to think for himself and to own the results. Above all, the process generates new perspective, encouraging decisions that are truly "out of the box." Very, very bold. As we see more clearly into the heart of the matter, solutions may arise that are very different from the organization's beliefs and assumptions about what to do or how to go about doing it. Fresh insights may run counter to what historical data suggest.

And let's face it, while everybody says they are looking for big ideas, in truth, the bigger the idea the more resistance it may create. By definition, big ideas are not tried-and-true; people who lack confidence (or, if you dare use the word, faith) easily find reasons why they won't work out in practice. They challenge, ignore, debate, analyze, find fault, push back. Resistance is a natural occurrence, but inspiring managers turn it to their advantage by actively engaging with the naysayers or enlisting them in finding an even better way. Keep them focused on the outcome; ask them to reflect *for themselves* on questions such as:

"What needs to happen?"
"How could we move forward?"
"Who could be involved?"

Easing the Group Decision Process

Conventional: Toiling	Step Up: Flowing
Each party keeps repeating basically the same position and supporting data, over and over again	Guide discussion so that each viewpoint is surfaced—but just once, with opportunity for clarification/elaboration
Debate goes in circles	Ask each person to consider what he/she finds surprising
You, or others, experience strong emotional reactions	Make room for creative tension. Probe what's itching.

High-Wire Key to Decisions That Inspire Confident Action: Reflect with Volition

The obvious can sneak up on us. It often drifts into our awareness quietly, even as a feeling that "something is missing"—as happened for the accounts payable manager we met at the beginning of this chapter. When we become aware of a nagging doubt, that's the time to slow down and pay attention. Something significant is about to become obvious through insight—ours, or that of our colleagues.

Rely, as well, on one other habit: a deep will or volition to keep moving forward. In other words, see to it that decisions are put into practice by always pushing ahead. Parse even the biggest dreams into a series of step-by-step actions.

Ultimately, having faith in one's own intuition is a hallmark of all great leaders. Our decisions may look risky since they are not necessarily relying on observable, tangible facts. But even though the ultimate outcome may not be known for months, action is facilitated by our optimism.

> The world we have made, as a result of the level of thinking we have done thus far, creates problems we cannot solve at the same level of thinking at which we created them.
>
> —Albert Einstein[2]

CHAPTER 5

Letting Go to Get Ahead

Key question: How do I inspire others to achieve goals using their own skill and ingenuity?

Just a couple of months after being promoted, Judy was already overloaded. She knew she should assign a portion of her work to her staff, but felt too new to be confident that they would get it done to the standards that had earned her promotion. In other words, she faced one of the most significant hurdles in the transition from "in the trenches" to "bigger picture": learning to delegate.

Judy's group had to ensure that materials for the monthly board of directors' meetings were ready, accurate, complete, and in the directors' hands a few days before each meeting. Talk about a moving target! Fifteen people on the board—just keeping track of their movements was a full-time endeavor. Complicating matters, each agenda item had an "owner" who was responsible for preparing the materials, having them reviewed by the CEO, and then making changes. The more important the topic, the more likely the owner would wait until the very last minute to get the materials to Judy's team. "I like to play 'beat the clock,'" is how one person saw it.

At first, Judy saw herself as the hub of the wheel, with each of her subordinates as a spoke. She insisted that everything passed through her hands with predictable consequences. As the old saying goes, "The bottleneck is always at the top of the bottle." By Judy's second board meeting, the fire drill was overwhelming.

"I'm at my wits' end," she told a friend. "My staff seems competent enough, but they aren't taking up the slack. Plus, it seems as though I have multiple jobs—getting my own work done and then making sure that my subordinates are doing theirs, too."

As she was taking a bath that evening, Judy realized that she had to trust her people. But how?

It's a question faced by everyone who moves up the management ladder. We know that delegation releases more constructive energy than anything else a manager can do. But delegation is hard to do—in part because a leader can never get out from under responsibility. As President Harry Truman so famously said, "The buck stops here."

But sharing responsibility is just one facet of delegation. It's actually a balancing act with three parts: authority, accountability, and responsibility. Often, they are treated as the same. Skillful managers know the difference— how to share responsibility, when to exercise or delegate authority, plus how to assign accountability. Consider, for example, the classic tale of young George Washington chopping down the cherry tree. The act was a problem because the boy did not have the *authority* to do it. When his father confronted him, George made no effort to shift the blame or make excuses, but said, "I cannot tell a lie. I cut down the cherry tree with my little hatchet." He was admirably *accountable*. But to be *responsible*, the lad would have gone one step farther: he would have planted a new tree to "make things right."

Balancing Power

Authority: the right to decide, to command, to make things happen. Without authority, a manager becomes a eunuch, for he does not have the ability to procreate—in other words, to produce the required results.
Accountability: answering for one's actions; taking appropriate blame (or credit). One who is accountable is, indeed, required to "stand and account" for outcomes under all circumstances.
Responsibility: taking necessary action, including, when necessary, making things right. The word literally means "able to respond"—not failing to act if able.

Assign Outcomes, Not Activities

The urge to hold the reins of authority tightly, as Judy experienced, is normal for newly promoted managers. Behind it is a fundamental uncertainty: "Will my subordinates really deliver?" It takes a leap of faith to believe that others not only have the capability to step up, but also the commitment to make whatever contribution is required. The manager's charge is to ensure that the staff has the skills and resources to get the job done within the required parameters. But let the staff *own the project.*

Without such faith, a vicious circle is created—the manager delegates in name only, so subordinates hold back and fail to deliver, thus seeming to validate the manager's lack of faith. All sorts of organizational hobgoblins take hold: micromanaging, doing the subordinate's job for him, confusion over roles, pointing the finger of blame, decision paralysis, and on and on. The impact on action, tone, and productivity can be debilitating. This is where a skillful manager distinguishes herself. Like a good parent, she places accountability for the outcome squarely on her lieutenants' shoulders while communicating a feeling of utter confidence in their competence.

The night that Judy saw that she needed to entrust her people, she decided to put the issue on the table. Next morning, she asked everyone on her team to come into the conference room. She began, a bit awkwardly: "First, I want to let everyone know how much I appreciate and value the hard work, dedication, and effort you put into these board meetings. And so far, so good— the CEO has been pleased that the meeting materials are ready in time and that the notes and follow-through happen so quickly. But we can't go on any longer doing this job the way we have always done it. We are burning out; I am overloaded. We risk missing key deadlines or making a serious error; that could be bad for the company and might make our boss look bad. So we are going to throw out the old cookbook and start fresh."

"Are you asking us for our ideas about how we can do this job better?" piped up Cheryl, one of the long-time staff members. "Yes, I am," replied Judy.

"Well, for a start, we never seem to have enough clarity about the agenda far enough in advance," Cheryl observed.

Judy stood up and said, "This has been very helpful. I'm going to the CEO's office right now and talk about next month's board agenda."

On her way down the hall, Judy was worried: "My team needs to see that I'm really serious about doing things differently. But how can I provide the clarity they want? The CEO doesn't clue me in, either. We're under the gun for every board meeting, and the problem starts with him! How can I change his behavior? What can I say to him?"

Then she had an insight. The CEO had been assigning *activities*, not *outcomes* to her, and she had mindlessly passed them on to the staff. Delegating the appropriate share of responsibility, accountability, and authority would be easy if she really understood what the CEO wanted. Once they were on the same page, she could give the staff a clear idea of the performance standard that they needed to meet. She could then assign *accountability* for each outcome along with the *authority* to achieve it.

Sustaining an objective, nondefensive stance, Judy let the CEO know what she needed. As she steadfastly insisted that he provide a picture of his purpose for each meeting, she made the switch from assigning activities to delegating accountabilities. At first, her team members were shocked. In fact, they tried to push the accountabilities back to her desk. But Judy stayed firm—continually pointing out that she expected them to accomplish the results.

Soon, team members were attacking problems with gusto and gaining confidence in their ability to take on more responsibility. They began to sense that there was something more at stake. The game they were playing was more about becoming really, really good at helping executives throughout the company prepare and run meetings—any meetings.

Judy also noticed that team members brought her a different kind of questions. Instead of asking her to check their work or to give them the solutions to issues, they asked for guidance in prodding other departments to meet key deadlines or keep commitments. These were the kinds of challenges that only a manager at Judy's level could resolve because they meant dealing with executives from others parts of the company. Instead of depleting all of her energy in checking each and every step along the way, now Judy could switch her focus to such bigger-picture roadblocks.

There was also a subtle change in the working relationships within the group. Judy's staff realized that joint accountability meant that they had to work more effectively together—share information, allow people to focus on getting their tasks done, volunteer to help when someone was falling behind.

When a manager is only paying lip service to delegation, employees are quick to see that the deeds don't match the words. They stop trying, waiting instead for their supervisor to call the shots. They forgo their inborn ability to access their ingenuity—insight plus common sense—and withdraw to the seemingly safe, to what has worked before.

But when people are, like Judy's team, sharing responsibility and authority by design, they are capable of achieving results more rapidly. Decisions, once made, are implemented quickly because everyone sees how the pieces fit together and, therefore, understands how to adjust his or her own activities. In other words, each person throughout the organization begins applying his or her own inner resources to accomplish the desired ends. Individuals lend their talents freely to this kind of collective enterprise.

The Manager's Role: Setting Context

In short, your job is *not* about having all the answers. It's about seeing the right questions to ask and posing them in a way that is energizing. Make the neutral query, "I have a question for you to consider," instead of the more pointed, "What do you mean by that?" Engage in dialogue that brings out fresh thinking—in yourself and, equally or even more important, in your team.

Essential to that kind of dialogue, and to successful delegation, is skill in clarifying context. A dream, objective, or goal that is expressed in fuzzy terms frustrates collective accomplishment. But when the goal is well articulated and the context clear, people have road signs that guide moment-to-moment actions. Context is clarified through an ongoing conversation about:

- what matters;
- what is possible, given what matters;
- what needs to be accomplished, given what is possible;
- how one contributes, given what needs to be accomplished.

These are simple guideposts, really—so simple that they are too often taken for granted. We may forget that people will gravitate toward variation since we all think differently. Thus, it may appear that people suit up to play basketball, only to find themselves on an ice rink because the game is hockey.

High-Wire Delegating

Conventional: Consternation	Step Up: Clear Context
Concerned about looking good	Connecting with others
Management = bottleneck	Energy toward the outcome
Focus on obstacles	Anticipate challenges
Tell or sell	Dialogue
Force decisions on the people most affected	Involve interested parties in finding solutions

By clarifying context before delegating, managers—like Judy—are able to keep teams moving in generally the same direction. When context is clear, individual efforts become complementary, even synergistic. As people focus on shared goals, the whole becomes greater than its parts.

Some managers recognize the contextual questions but try to dictate the answers—to *tell* the organization what to do. In such cases, we often see feelings of confusion ("I hear the words, but don't understand the meaning"), compliance ("I don't agree with what you're saying, but I won't argue with you"), or coercion ("Pay me enough, and I'll do what you ask even though I am not happy about it").

Other managers come up with the answers and then try to *sell* the organization. They marshal intellectual arguments about why this is the best course of action. This may lead to passive resistance ("Wait a while, and this will blow over"), obstinacy ("You'll have to prove that there's something in this for me"), or apprehension ("Whoa! I don't see how we'll ever be able to do this").

In contrast, the manager attuned to the wisdom that exists within all people views the dialogue about context as an ongoing opportunity for everyone to gain insight, find perspective, and internalize concepts that will simplify everyday decisions and actions. The organization becomes self-defining (the answers are owned widely) as well as self-correcting (based on the deep understanding that comes from engaged involvement). Managers, peers, and subordinates stand on common ground and have the resiliency to keep things on track.[1]

The Ultimate in Delegation: Choosing Your Successor

An effective leader knows she has only two measures of success. The obvious: tangible outcomes achieved during her own tenure. But equally important is her legacy, the further progress made after she's gone. Therefore, the ultimate act of delegation is choosing one's successor: literally handing over the reins.

Johnson & Johnson, for example, has a policy that the retiring CEO really steps aside—off the board of directors, banished to an office far away from the executive corridor, privileges revoked except for a single administrative assistant. "Don't call us, we'll call you" is the unspoken rule.

Two leadership transitions at Johnson & Johnson are instructive. When Jim Burke took over from Richard Sellars in 1976, the company's revenues had broken $1 billion; when Burke stepped down 13 years later, J&J's profits had just reached $1 billion; and in 2002, when Ralph Larsen retired after his 13-year tenure, the company's market capitalization was $180 billion, a nearly 13-fold increase from $14 billion value in 1989.

What's particularly noteworthy is that these three men were very different types—Sellars was a sales guy, Burke marketing, Larsen operations. But each accomplished outstanding results during his own tenure *and* set the stage for his successor to accomplish even more. How did that happen?

Certainly, the stature of the company and its strong decentralized culture meant that good people were available. More important, however, each of these men was able to put aside his own ego and choose a successor very different from himself in experience and skills.

The common denominator that these leaders shared was a deep, unwavering belief in human capacity. In addition, all three assumed that the leader's job is to create conditions so that this potential can be expressed. So while they considered objective factors—such as track record, background, technical competence—ultimately, they based selection of the next chief on a gut feeling that the designated successor would be able to nurture the intangible aspects of human accomplishment.

J&J's long success was influenced by other internal and external factors, including market conditions and technological advances. But what allowed the company to outperform the competition was the ability of its leaders to sustain a culture poised to take maximum advantage of opportunities.

The Upward Steps of Management

For managers stepping up to ever-increasing levels of responsibility and the simultaneously increasing need to delegate outcomes more broadly, it can be helpful to think about leadership at three levels. We are not talking about the multitude of reporting levels that may exist inside your company. Rather, we are pointing to distinctions that mark key transitions as managers enhance their leadership (figure 5.1).

Leaders of Self

These are passionate, energetic people who make strong individual contributions, who are diligent about their work, and who strive to succeed. They have earned a reputation for getting things done. They solve their own problems, often with little support. Internally motivated, they bring a vibrancy to

FIGURE 5.1

As managers become more confident in their leadership, their focus shifts. Ultimately, their confidence transforms them to "leaders of leaders"—no longer the central battery from which others draw energy, but part of a synergistic endeavor.

Challenges to Leaders of Self

Often unaware that others have not developed their gifts to the same degree, *leaders of self* must see that they actually do, in fact, manage— primarily by being good examples for others, the ultimate in *leading by influence.*

The rest of the organization must learn to value this form of leading from the "bottom." Strong, forceful personalities tend to get the spotlight; quiet, competent individual contributors are too often overlooked.

work as they accomplish objectives. They don't ask for much recognition, unlike high-maintenance peers who may come forward with inane interruptions.

Exemplifying the *leader of self* is the former director of marketing at Gunn Partners, Donna DuBose. She makes things happen without fanfare, direction, or intervention. Her boss never has to question her judgments or follow up on her actions. People love having her on their teams and find it a pleasure just being around her. On conference calls she is often the one who keeps the conversation on track and ensures that desired outcomes are clear in everyone's minds.

Surely, people like Donna exist throughout your institution. Perhaps their most important talent is that they access their innate wisdom easily; answers seem to have a way of coming to them when needed. And they have the internal motivation to take action by allowing this inner voice to guide their moment-to-moment steps. These are two of the fundamental building blocks that all great managers possess.

Leaders of Others

On the next distinct level are the leaders of groups, teams, or projects. These middle managers, as they are often called, are the sinews of every organization. They hold the well-being, growth, and accomplishments of others

Questions for Leaders of Others

Not: "What do my direct reports need to do" so that they accomplish results
Instead: "What needs doing for my subordinates" so that we all can be successful

foremost in their thoughts and act accordingly. *Leaders of others* help everyone tap his own ingenuity. Thus, they unleash the collective power that comes from teams working effectively.

A good example of this kind of leader is the sergeant who guided his troops by seeing to their needs, as opposed to looking out for his own well-being. Every morning, when it was his job to escort the privates to the canteen for breakfast, he took the last position in line. Most of the other drill instructors went to the head. As one of his charges recounts, "He did this knowing full well that all the good bread and marmalade would be gone by the time he got to the front of the line. But when he led us in the field, he never had to yell and shout—we did more for him than for all the other sergeants put together."

It is not hard to see that this kind of interest, care, and attention generates enthusiasm in any group, no matter how hard-bitten. Many movies—from *Gandhi* to *Saving Private Ryan*—illustrate this point. The leader does not hold himself apart from others, but rather acknowledges the connectedness of us all. He generates the feeling of being part of something larger than oneself that sustains sacrifice in the face of challenges, and optimism in the face of adversity.

Leaders of Leaders—Managing from Within

- See that the primary task is to release and nurture the leadership in others
- Ensure that the tone of the organization is upbeat, that people feel free to speak their minds
- Rely on creativity, freshness, ease, warmth, and grace to help people feel confident and grounded
- Show by their conduct that everyone has inner resources that are always up to the challenge

---

Leaders of Leaders

Managers simply cannot do their best when the boss is trying to do their jobs as well as his own. Usually, this behavior is unintended. Becoming a *leader of leaders* means, foremost, stepping back from the action. Unlike the *leader of others*, who keeps the controls firmly in hand, the *leader of leaders* does not step in and take over. Often, stepping up means giving up something that one dearly loved doing—for a skier, no longer skiing in the deep powder. The denial is purely voluntary, so it takes real strength of will to step back.

In place of familiar tasks, what do leaders of leaders really do? Roger Enrico describes conversations with Wayne Calloway, the former CEO of PepsiCo and Enrico's mentor, as two hours of him rambling and Calloway listening, punctuated by a few questions. Somehow, Enrico always came away with the answers he was seeking, never understanding exactly how this transpired.[2] Perhaps what Calloway knew was to trust the innate power that the other leaders in his company, Enrico included, possessed to find their own insights.

Leaders of leaders demonstrate that they "walk the talk" by taking on the few, usually very difficult, tasks that no one else is positioned to do or, perhaps, sees the need to do. And they are not interested in creating followers who mimic them. Quite the contrary. They seek out people who are independent-minded and on the path of deepening their own consciousness about what it means to lead.

High-Wire Key to Delegating: Get Your Ego Out of the Way

Managers must trust that things will work out. We do that in part because, through experience, we've seen people rise to the occasion when given the chance. But, more important, we do it because we *know* that every individual has innate resources of intuition, insight, creativity, wisdom. We're so accustomed to handling tasks, however, that we jump to *doing* before we think.

To have a profound impact, managers need merely to point in a direction, perhaps by asking a question, and then to engage others in the process of exploration until clarity and certainty emerge. How employees feel about assignments depends, in large part, on how much of the manager's personal ego is invested, versus how much he is pointing toward a common benefit.

People with highly self-centered thinking who end up at the top of a team or an organization create chaos. Their need to dominate, to control, causes subordinates to just get by, meet the minimum requirements.[3] The more they do what they want, the harder it is for them to enlist others' help. A manager with a big ego is a bit like a mobile home being pulled along the highway without warning flags. He careens down the lane blocking other traffic, perhaps causing an accident.

As we've seen, Judy's team challenged her on this very point. Right up front they said, "OK, we hear that you want us to be more accountable. But is that to our benefit, or yours? Are you willing to change? Are you willing to stand up to the big boss? Give us some evidence."

When managers direct their willpower toward collective accomplishment, they find it easy to enlist the thinking of others to help achieve the common cause. Motivating others is less about telling people what to do and more about helping them tap their passion, understand their purpose, honor what they uniquely can contribute, and find the place where they best fit.

A little humility goes a long way to smoothing out the rough edges of delegation.

> As for the best leaders, the people do not notice their existence.
> The next best, the people honor and praise.
> The next, the people fear; and the next, the people hate.
> When the best leader's work is done, the people say, "We did it ourselves."
>
> —Lao Tzu, Chinese philosopher, c.604 B.C.

SECOND PRECEPT

Strong Connections Begin with Respect for Separate Thinking

CHAPTER 6

Job One—Setting the Right Tone

Key question: How do I create feelings of enthusiasm *and* get
the nitty-gritty tasks accomplished?

Shortly before her 27th birthday, Betsy stepped up to her first management
role: overseeing a staff of 11 (all considerably older than she) in producing a trade magazine. After one restless night, she came into work glowering
and grumbling, tossing off curt hellos on the way to her office. Within 20
minutes, she became aware that staffers who had been smiling were now
scowling. Banter and laughter had stopped. The light in the office even seemed
darker.

"Did I do that?" Betsy wondered. "Did my bad mood infect everyone
else? Is that the real power of a manager?"

Yes, yes, and, with all due humility, yes.

The mood shadow cast by a manager is a long one. Don't you check
with the boss's admin to find out if she is in a good mood before asking
for that raise? Next time you initiate a conference call in a bad mood, just
watch what happens. We predict you'll hear painfully long lags in conversation. Notice that issues are sidestepped; watch as people find reasons to
bail out.

Inspiring managers head off such problems by staying closely attuned to
moods. They know that their "bad hair day" can easily cause associates to feel
tension and stress. They know not to push if they wake up on the wrong side
of the bed, or if a meeting turns dispirited. People simply don't do their best

work when they are in a low mood. While we may take that statement for granted, too often we fail to act accordingly!

Good moods, too, can be catching. When we feel positive and light-hearted or when we hear others express humor or warmth, we know that a great deal can be accomplished easily and quickly. A lighthearted workplace tends to be not only less stressful, but also more productive. The *Harvard Business Review* recently took note of research under way at the University of Michigan Business School: "they are finding that employee happiness really does pay. It's beginning to look as if a positive workplace atmosphere is worth developing, and not merely for its own sake; it may be the foundation of true organizational success."[1]

To put it simply: job #1 for managers is to pay attention to tone—that pitch of language plus body posture and movement that expresses meaning eloquently.

"Just Give Us a Safe Haven..."

Mike, president of a manufacturer of electronic components, walked into a meeting of his sales managers and found them laughing about a humorous incident at one of their best customers. He blew up. "What's so funny!" he exclaimed. "I'm not paying you to have fun on the job. And let me assure you that I am not finding your results anything to laugh at." Oops. The meeting went downhill from there; people went through the motions, but nothing substantive was accomplished as they fluctuated between resentfulness and fear.

Mike failed to see the chilling effect of his words. Sally, one of the most productive account managers, voiced her feelings over a cup of coffee later that day.

"You know I respect Mike and actually like spending time with him one-on-one. He has taught me more about selling and relationship management than any boss ever; truly, I am grateful for that. But he is always so serious and gets upset so easily that I get depressed coming into work. It feels like my nose is being held to the grindstone, and I never know what to expect," Sally said.

"I know that I have to meet my quarterly numbers and do my part to help Mike reach his. That is a given. That's why I am in sales; performance is 100% tangible. Either I deliver the results, or I don't. No excuses.

"I just wish Mike would trust my internal motivation and give us all a safe haven from the gorillas we face every day on the road. For my own peace of mind, I think I need to start looking for a new job."

True to her word, Sally was gone in six months. Mike never understood why.

The Surprising Usefulness of Emotion

We must be aware of the *mood* of the people in meetings, in customer interactions, on the phone, at all times. Equally important, we must pay attention to how *we* feel—for that gives us important clues to the quality of our thinking. Every feeling is linked to a thought: anxious feelings, insecure thoughts; angry feelings, thoughts of betrayal; sad feelings, thoughts of disappointment; happy feelings, thoughts of pride or achievement; excited feelings, optimistic thoughts, and so on. As soon as we *see* our thoughts, we have new possibilities for setting tone. We need no longer be controlled by old patterns, moving through our days on emotional autopilot.

The High-Wire Thought Continuum

Conventional: Burning out	Step Up: Resiliency
Frustration	Humor
Pessimism	Possibility
Worry	Wonder
Anxiety	Anticipation
Annoyance	Empathy
Insecurity	Eagerness to learn
Defensiveness/blame	Benefit-of-the-doubt
Jealousy	Gratitude
Anger	Puzzlement
Resentment	Forgiveness

Unfortunately, the mood at many, if not most, companies works against us. Worry can paralyze us from taking even the most obvious action. Insecurity can cause us to make the same mistakes over and over again. Defensiveness can shift the blame while the underlying issue never gets resolved. Jealousy can isolate people who are supposed to be on the same team. Resentment can limit contributions. Pessimism can turn minor issues into major roadblocks (figure 6.1).

A stressful atmosphere is nothing more nor less than a corporate bad mood. Its cost is not always obvious at first glance, but goes well beyond the visible manifestations of sick days or employee turnover, reaching into the nexus of every human interaction. As people become withdrawn or short-tempered, the goodwill that lubricates human interaction stops working. Misunderstandings build into conflict. Bosses see no other way to get the job done than by promulgating and enforcing rules to govern behavior. As a result, they have endless meetings to bring people together who don't even want to be in the same room, tinker with incentives to motivate the right

Positive Tone is the Precursor of Better Outcomes

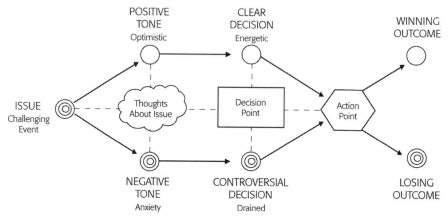

FIGURE 6.1

Adversity happens; managers can't change that. But the tone—the feeling or mood—we maintain as we react to the situation does shape response.

actions, yell to vent their own frustration, or fire the worst malcontents to make public examples.

Common sense tells us this is counterproductive. So why does gloominess prevail far more often than cheerfulness? Why is the most common managerial assumption that we have to be serious in order to be productive—variations on the "stop laughing and get back to work" theme?

One reason is that many of us live with unexamined assumptions about our jobs. Consider some common phrases: we "put on our game faces" when we walk through the office door; we start our weeks on "blue Mondays" and end saying, "Thank God it's Friday," or sometimes admonish co-workers to "stop clowning around."

When the Team Is in the Dumpster

Customers were complaining. In Kemp's accounting team, work was backing up. He had brought a tried-and-true model—which had worked in his two previous jobs—to his new group at Hewlett Packard. His HR person had quickly implemented the concept: a team-based structure in which individuals made most decisions without relying on managers to tell them what to do. Many employees embraced the refreshing change from the "command and control" mentality of Kemp's predecessor. And most of the new team leaders liked Kemp personally; they found his enthusiasm and energy uplifting.

Yet the group was having trouble "getting" the team concept. An elusive obstacle was in the way. What was puzzling was that some teams were thriving while others were stuck in first gear, going nowhere fast.

One day, while driving into work, Kemp thought about John Madden, the former football coach turned announcer. He always seemed upbeat. Kemp realized that some of his teams were really having a good time at work—and they were the ones experiencing the best performance. "Maybe that is the secret," Kemp thought. "I'll just work on helping lift the spirits of the dour teams and see if that makes a difference."

He began to focus his energy on improving the tone of the poorly performing groups. For example, he conducted meetings about the importance of job enjoyment. He asked team members to do simple exercises to clear mental baggage—he had them reflect on the question, "Is there anything I need to do so that I can concentrate on my work today?" And he reminded them to appreciate the efforts of their teammates.

In just a matter of days, things began to change for the better. Of course, a few personnel changes were required—people who "just don't enjoy" teamwork were moved to different roles. But as quickly as the mood improved, so did performance.

Who decided that being professional meant being glum? Just because we have serious responsibilities, must we take *ourselves* so darn seriously? Educators know that when children are happy, they are learning.[2] But something happens to us when we begin working. There's an ingrained thought that we are engaging in "serious business." Certainly, business has never seemed more difficult, our challenges more risky, our problems more complex. And that's precisely why it's more important than ever to make room for humor in the workplace.

High-Wire Tone

Conventional: "Serious Business"	Step Up: "Let 'em Loose"
"Do or die"	"We can work it out"
"Nose to the grindstone"	"Whistle while you work"
Disagreements are personal	Respect each individual's thinking
"Keep 'em in line"	"We're all doing the best we can"

Humor as Tone-Setting Strategy

Corporate moods, like individual moods, represent thinking that is stuck on a theme. Negative thoughts can churn on, spiraling the mood ever lower. Caught in a thought loop, we have a harder and harder time surfacing insights and working together to find solutions.

The Right Time for Humor

- When you're busy-minded and feeling uncreative
- When you're stuck and can't make a decision
- When you're angry and making other people defensive
- In short, whenever you're in a pattern that sets a negative tone

---

Humor can open a valuable doorway—from entrenched positions to a change in thinking. Nobody can get stuck in an unproductive thought pattern—anger, worry, anxiety, frustration—if she's laughing. When we laugh, we've allowed ourselves to be surprised, to look at things differently. Laughter affirms that we see more than one reality. If there are more than one, which is "right"?

Laughter comes from the space between thoughts. It's a bursting out not just of sound, but also of feeling. Laughter loosens everything up, shakes asunder the chains we impose by our expectations, softens our boundaries. Even the most minute lightening of ego opens up wonderful possibilities!

We are not speaking about the forced humor that comes at someone's expense. Comments that poke fun at a person's foibles or ridicule behaviors can damage anyone's sense of security.

Then, too, humor that comes from a stance of "I'm going to make you laugh so you'll like me," is less universal, and less effective. Humor works best when it's organic—it wells up and flows freely because we are secure, grounded.

Taking the Sting Out of Mistakes

Jay Schweppe is one of the most successful real-estate brokers in the country. In good times and bad, he captures a 50–60% share of his market, more than three times that of his next competitor. In fact, his office in Montclair, New Jersey, has been featured as a front-page story in the *Wall Street Journal*. Jay is famous for giving speeches extolling his management techniques.[3]

Every Wednesday Jay has a one-hour, all-staff meeting. It's a chance for him to remind people of the company's philosophy and make course corrections. But in tone and substance, it feels like a night at the Comedy Club. You can't help but laugh—to the point that sometimes it actually hurts. Jay's weekly meetings have become can't miss events, sometimes with 60 or 70 people crowding into a room meant to hold 40.

His right-hand person, Denise, the brokerage president, is a pretty serious individual. No nonsense. Tough minded. But she sees the wisdom in Jay's methods. "By pointing out the absurdity in what we are doing, Jay helps us see the flaws in our actions that are obviously working against us. Errors in our deepest assumptions are brought to light. He points out defects in our thinking that make us less effective. But we never feel bad about it. We know he wants the best for us and that his examples are never mean-spirited.

"The genius is that a good belly laugh about an incredibly stupid action clears the air. Takes the sting out of the mistake. Leaves the lesson without the bad feeling. And, boy, does it help everyone go into the most important part of the week with a burst of energy!"

Lost in Thought

By tending tone, managers lubricate team interactions. In other words, they sustain rapport—a feeling of mutual goodwill. Rapport doesn't mean we have to like everyone, or that everyone has to like us. The first step to rapport is simply remembering that each person brings to every conversation his or her own set of expectations, perceptions, perspectives. Too often we assume that if someone disagrees with us, they must be stupid, uninformed, insulting—or any of a number of uncomfortable adjectives. Or we become insecure, fearing that we might have missed something.

> **Rapport Step 1** Recognize that we're all trying to do the best we can, based on different realities shaped by thinking that looks *absolutely real* to each thinker.

We often take disagreements personally. Since what we think is "real" to us, surely the other person *must* see it our way, too. Why are they refusing to cooperate; why are they being so stubborn? So there we are in the middle of a conversation, distracted by bad feelings. Or we're thinking about our own agenda, focused on what we want the other person to say or do.

The fact is that the other person is just operating from a different viewpoint than we are, a different way of looking at things, a different set of thoughts that look absolutely real to him. Even if his words sound like a personal attack, the root of the problem is an ordinary fact of life: we are all doing the best that we can to communicate from perspectives shaped by what looks real to us, and uniquely to us.

All tension in any relationship stems from this single problem: each of us is locked in an isolation booth shaped by our thoughts. The more we are absorbed in and by our own thoughts without realizing it, the harder it is for us to sustain rapport–to stay connected with other people, to listen and interact.

> **Rapport Step 2** Be aware that thoughts can run away from anybody, seemingly spinning out of our control. Someone may seem self-centered, adversarial. But don't make matters worse by taking his tantrum personally.

We could see the pattern in such quiz shows as the Comedy Channel's *Win Ben Stein's Money*. In the climax of each show, Ben Stein, himself, went head-to-head with a contestant to see which of them could correctly answer the most questions in 60 seconds. Ben was serious about wanting to win, but everything else about his program poked fun at the quiz show genre. The two opponents sat in separate booths; the one who would go second was given earphones so that he or she couldn't hear the questions–just as in such classics as *The $64,000 Question*. But since it was Ben's show, his isolation booth had a cushy armchair, an Oriental rug on the floor, an antique clock, a fine painting. The contestant's booth had patched walls, a bare stool, a clock with a broken face, trash on the floor. Ben's booth was resplendent, his opponent's austere. Yet the degree of comfort was irrelevant, for each was equally isolated. Hearing only what was fed through their earphones, they lost the freedom to choose what they paid attention to.

All of us are caught, to greater or lesser degrees, in our own isolation booths. On a large scale, this phenomenon takes its toll in blood: how many people died this very week because they have different religious beliefs? But we're all in thrall to our thoughts every day. The proof is no farther away than the next conference call: how long can you go without your mind wandering?

The point is that each of us is living our own reality, shaped by our thoughts brought to life as a feeling that, in turn, powers our behavior. Two people or 20 people involved in the same interaction will have 2 or 20 perspectives about what is happening. Therein lies one of the greatest challenges for leaders everywhere.

What's the *Real* Problem?

Bev was steaming. Operations had let her down...again. She had promised that the order for her biggest customer was going to be out the door by the end of the day; yet when she came into her office the next morning, there was the e-mail. Nothing had been shipped. Zip. Nada. She wanted to throw something. She marched down the hall to see Jeff, the Operations VP and her boss.

As she reached Jeff's door, Bev caught a glimpse of him sitting in his chair, looking stricken. Furious as she was, her hand paused on the doorknob. She flashed on the thought, "That poor man, he looks as though the weight of the world is on his shoulders."

Bev found herself stepping over the threshold and saying, "Jeff, you look terrible. Is there anything I can do for you?" She wondered where those words came from since she was still fuming inside. But the power of compassion had momentarily allowed Bev to be fully *present*. In that state of mind, it was obvious that yelling at Jeff was going to accomplish little more than add to her frustration. It certainly wasn't going to fix anything.

Jeff saw that Bev was being genuine; her offer to help was real. In the next few minutes he revealed that he had gotten off the phone with her customer just before Bev walked in. He was asking if Jeff could add yet another "minor" custom design feature before the unit went out the door. This buyer had been making these changes on virtually everything they had shipped for months, altering specs right up to the last minute, way past policy guidelines, seriously disrupting operations and hurting productivity.

"Sounds as though we should fire this customer," Bev said, astonishing herself. Jeff was equally amazed: "You mean you would actually tell our best customer to take a hike?"

As she walked back to her office, Bev realized that later she would need to revisit why she had gotten so upset. But she marveled at how different the conversation would have been if she had decided to stay righteously angry instead of being present with what was going on for Jeff. Sure, Bev was angry as she walked down the hall. But she had the presence of mind to realize that she had a choice when she opened Jeff's door. She could have acted from anger; instead, she chose empathy.

Bev realized that Jeff had been doing the best job he knew and not bothering Bev about a difficult character at an important customer. Now, instead of allowing someone to bully her company, Bev had the information to work toward a solution at the level it should have been handled all along.

Rapport Begins at Home

Whatever is going on with the other person, we must find even the tiniest spot in ourselves that respects his thinking. Resist the temptation to try to make the other person see things more rationally, more reasonably. Insistence on "right versus wrong" can create an even tougher barrier between him and us. Instead, help the person lean toward, and on, the piece of himself that is, always, connected to common sense.

Rapport Step 3 Be patient, kind, and compassionate to *yourself* when you make mistakes or fail to meet

your own expectations. Your lucidity and
your ability to establish open lines of communication depend on it.

Graceful managers know that the key to *group* tone is attending to *our
own* mental well-being. See the other person not as an adversary, nor as an
obstacle; not as a problem, nor as the person giving orders; not the person
holding up payment of the invoice, nor the person thwarting the sale. But as a
human being, trying to do the best he can, trying to overcome his insecurities—
just as we all are. Something they say touches us; we become curious about
what they mean.

High-Wire Key to Motivating Employees: Foster a Safe Environment Through Tone

By paying attention to tone, we foster a safe environment in which our teams
can stay mentally loose—thereby doing their best thinking and their best
work. A buoyant tone encourages enormous productivity. Even the most difficult or repetitive task is made easier when we make light of it instead of
reminding ourselves how hard it is. Sometimes when people are just fooling
around, they can produce astonishing results. At times like these, it seems that
the manager's only task is to point toward the proper goal so that positive
energy is channeled in the right direction. Tone becomes the solid foundation
for management that motivates teams without sapping the manager's own
energy.

We are pointing to common sense executive leadership. As a manager,
you own the tone, the mood that is present. Attend to your own mental well-
being first. When you are clear, calm, quiet, focused, feeling good or even
happy, eager to begin the day or the meeting, that feeling will be contagious.
Then help others clear the cobwebs. Connect them to a purpose larger than
their own. Remind them that work is about the "we," not the "me." Gently
freeing employees from their habitual thoughts goes a long way toward a
highly productive workplace.

You control the gravity on this planet. Lighten up!

—Fortune Cookie

CHAPTER 7

Sales and Meetings

Key question: How can I strengthen interpersonal relationships so that I can meet goals?

Richard was shaken, even angry, after his largest customer complained bitterly about the service he was receiving. Richard's whole team was working overtime; how could the customer be so unfair?

"What's going on?" Richard's manager asked: "I know he has a new boss, so is he feeling a bit pressured?" Richard blinked. "Hmm," he mused, speaking more slowly and quietly. "Maybe he is worried about making a good first impression."

One moment in his customer's shoes and Richard's thinking shifted. He didn't know specifics of his customer's pressures—could be the new boss or maybe he just woke up on the wrong side of bed. But merely by staying open to feelings, Richard was genuinely touched by the all-too-human condition of losing one's bearings. No longer taking the customer's tongue-lashing personally, even though it sounded personal at the time, Richard dropped his anger. He realized that he could reestablish connection just by letting the customer sense that he would be listening with a sincere desire to understand. In short, Richard got a new perspective on the basis of stronger relationships that we introduced in chapter 6: rapport.

It's "sales theory 101": before conducting any business—phone call, meeting, presentation—establish rapport. Ask about the family; tell a joke; talk about last night's sports events. Show that you're "one of the guys." Recall a shared experience, perhaps a golf outing, to reaffirm a bond.

But that's not enough to sustain the kind of affinity that achieves great results no matter how circumstances change. Instead of focusing on making others feel good *about us,* we need to establish a warm feeling that allows them to feel comfortable and confident *in themselves.* True rapport is less about sharing *experiences* and more about creating shared *meaning.*

"I could tell that the salesman had my best interests at heart—he was more interested in my success than in winning my business," one High-Wire customer observes. "Somehow his feeling of support gave me the confidence to take on a very challenging goal." His experience demonstrates that the stronger our rapport with customers (and with our staff members), the more *they* accomplish. What makes rapport powerful is the way a human connection clears both parties' mental cobwebs. And that strengthens the business relationship where it creates the most value (figure 7.1).

This way of looking at rapport transforms the conventional models. We used to believe that the best way to orchestrate a sales call was to spend a few minutes building rapport (i.e., telling stories so that they'd like us), with the

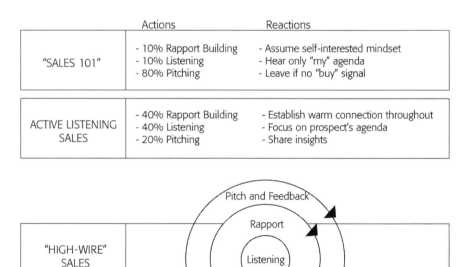

	Actions	Reactions
"SALES 101"	- 10% Rapport Building - 10% Listening - 80% Pitching	- Assume self-interested mindset - Hear only "my" agenda - Leave if no "buy" signal
ACTIVE LISTENING SALES	- 40% Rapport Building - 40% Listening - 20% Pitching	- Establish warm connection throughout - Focus on prospect's agenda - Share insights
"HIGH-WIRE" SALES	Pitch and Feedback Rapport Listening	

FIGURE 7.1

Rapport and listening are merely tools in conventional sales models, but the pulse-beat of conversations that move minds.

lion's share of the time devoted to our pitch, culminating in "asking for the order." In High-Wire sales conversations we keep building rapport until we sense a comfortable feeling, then gently begin exploring the customer's agenda. As she talks, we listen for common interests and connections to our purpose. At some point, sharing these will allow the conversation to progress naturally. Finally, it will become clear when to summarize the obvious conclusions and next steps (which may include writing up the order).

What transforms the High-Wire sales conversation is switching rapport from a door-opening technique to the pulse-beat of our interactions. Make the conversation an evolving loop of sharing-insights-and-getting-feedback, supported by reflective listening throughout.

A Master at Building Relationships

Barry Rand, the former president of Xerox (and subsequent CEO for Avis), was renowned as a "master marketer." His secret?

"I just went to our customers and listened to them talk about their needs. And then I went to our engineers and sales staffs and listened to what they were saying about our products and services. Putting two and two together, I was able to focus on whatever seemed most obvious, and then I had us take the appropriate action."

So simple, but so amazingly powerful. Just a question of plain common sense, according to Barry.

Upon meeting him, what jumps out is his ability to quickly establish rapport. He has Bill Clinton's knack of connecting, of giving you the feeling that his complete attention is concentrating on what *you* are saying. That he truly wants to understand *your* point. That he has all the time in the world to hear *you* out.

In other words, sales—of products, services, or even ideas—require meaningful connections. And the only true obstacle to greater effectiveness is our own thinking. When any of us give too much credit to our own beliefs and assumptions, we risk becoming like the fairy-tale emperor with no clothes—we shut out voices that are trying, often with great respect, to help us see a different picture. Through isolationist thinking, we create divisions; we put ourselves on one side and "them" on the other. We define situations using a set of right/wrong assumptions, consider options as being either/or, and then fight to the death to defend our "right answer."

The more effective stance is genuine goodwill. The way to establish such feelings is, as Richard discovered at the start of this chapter, by working from the inside, out. We diffuse wariness when we make a call or chair a meeting from this mindset.

Meetings of the Minds—Is There Any Other Kind?

Consider a typical scenario. The manager is faced with an underperforming unit and calls a meeting of its five top people. Having already analyzed the problem and devised several solutions, the leader is now thinking about the best way to sell his ideas to the others.

As the meeting begins, tension pervades the room. Everyone knows that something important is at stake; they feel threatened, even resentful. The manager dives right into the topic, not pausing for a moment to greet people, check in with the mood, or even ensure that the room is not too hot or cold. He begins by asserting his convictions strongly. The agenda grinds along. Fearful thoughts cause people to react defensively; angry thoughts spark arguments over trivial points; anxious thoughts evoke claims that nothing, not even the simplest changes, could ever work. The manager, already committed to his predetermined solution, becomes more forceful, slipping over the line from *selling* to *telling*.

As the meeting ends, people are spent. At best, the manager has gained a partial victory. But nobody's heart is really behind the decision, so people expect that the journey will be difficult. Resistance will likely spring up again and again.

Sound familiar? We've all been in too many meetings like this one! If that manager understood the role of *thinking*, things might turn out very different.

How High-Wire Managers Conduct Meetings

Conventional: Information	Step Up: Reflection
Dive right into the agenda	Build a nice feeling, then begin working
Convey news, policy, etc.	Explore questions; listen for concerns
Carefully edit what can be said	Surface "unmentionable" topics matter-of-factly, without emotional charge
Impart own knowledge; assert convictions	Nurture collective intelligence to generate fresh insights

First, give priority to the emotional pulse of the meeting. Start by making sure that your own thoughts are steady; that your mental well-being is high enough to support a positive, optimistic direction. Take a moment to welcome people. Allow them a few minutes to decompress from whatever was engaging their minds the moment before they walked through the door. And don't shortchange simple gestures to help people connect with each other. For example, express appreciation for each person—highlighting small but meaningful contributions. Whatever technique you use, begin the business of the meeting only when you sense the human feelings are warm and supportive. (Laughter is one wonderful signal that the rapport is solid enough to proceed.)

So what happens when the purpose of the meeting is to address something very negative, highly charged? Or when the feeling in the room is tense; people are uptight? Be extra considerate. Find a way to exhibit kindness. Remember that no matter how rampant the mental turmoil, negative thinking softens in the face of genuine care and concern. Anyone can regain mental balance in the blink of an eye. Changing the course of a difficult meeting is less challenging for managers who remember that low moods are merely manifestations of fearful thoughts.

Pay attention to tone—push when the mood is constructive, call a break when feelings take a turn for the worse. No more difficult, really, than driving a high performance car across a mountain pass in the winter: go faster on clear straightaways; downshift to negotiate icy hairpin turns.

Take as many steps forward as possible, allowing the energy in the meeting to mark progress and guide you. And when you sense that people have given their best, call it quits.

Meetings with high levels of rapport energize every attendee—including the manager who runs them. Because they shift perspective from personal concerns, such meetings allow the group to tackle even seemingly intractable challenges. People who rarely speak out in groups may be encouraged to contribute as unmentionable topics surface in a matter-of-fact way. Collective intelligence unearths pragmatic solutions beyond what any individual could ever hope to achieve alone. Feelings of solidarity become tangible, a sound basis for the work to come.

All the manager really needs to do is to master the art of *reflective listening*, in which agreeing or disagreeing with someone else's ideas is much less important than truly *seeing* from their perspective. That's the core competency underneath rapport. Reflective listening liberates us from concerns about how we look to others, how we'll deal with the stack of work on our desk, or where we need to be in 30 minutes. It clears our minds so that we can truly be responsive to what is happening moment to moment, and to the people with whom we are relating.

It's Not What We Say, It's How We Listen

Too many teachers of listening techniques send earnest acolytes down the wrong path. They tell us what to do: "*I* must exert effort to control *my* behavior; *I* must pay extra attention to *my* thought processes; *I* must increase *my* level of activity in order to hear what someone else is saying."

But the mental gymnastics of trying to concentrate on words actually has little to do with the art of listening. Ironically, the harder we try to remember each word, the more we are prone to habits that distance us from the speaker. We focus on *content*, taking notes (mental or actual) while the other person is talking.

As we analyze what they're saying, we're likely to look for those statements that bolster our point of view, or for ammunition to use in our own argument. While they are batting their yes, we are winding up our no. We may simply wait for the other person to take a breath so that we can take over the conversation.

In the middle of a typical pitch-and-hit disagreement, instead of delivering a rebuttal to Debra's logic, Terry took a breath and said, "Wait a minute. You have a point there." She was already drawing breath to deliver her next argument; Terry's switch caught her off guard, literally took her breath away. All at once, Debra felt off-balance, unsure what to say next, even a bit abashed at how emotional she'd become. "I got what I wanted," Debra mused later. "But I walked away feeling that Terry had somehow trumped me. Even though I'd won, I felt that he was more powerful."

At first, it may be hard to grasp the notion that we may understand what people are saying a lot better by focusing on feeling more than content. When we listen for feeling, we experience conversation as something that creates a sense of connectedness. What then becomes obvious is how our own thoughts interfere with our ability to listen deeply. The greater our own mental activity, the less understanding we gain.

High-Wire Listening

Conventional: Focus on Content	Step Up: Focus on Feeling
Taking notes	Noticing tone
Eager to answer back	Patient, calm
Looking for ammunition to bolster our argument	Asking clarifying questions
Assuming expectations/intent	Recognizing different perspectives

So how do we become masters of listening? As we've seen in our discussion of rapport in chapter 6, we have a better chance of connecting when we pay due respect to the thinking that drives us toward separation.

1. First, we remember that our own mental clutter creates insecurity. As we stop focusing on our internal rap and become truly curious about

what others are trying to convey, we automatically start listening more reflectively.

2. When we are open, others respond in kind; they are much more willing to share with us.

3. And as they talk about what looks real to them, we allow ourselves to connect and, perhaps, be inspired. We pay less attention to what we already know and start looking for fresh insights. Since our minds continually produce thoughts, why get attached to any particular notion? Thoughts are like subway trains: another one will be along in a minute.

Nancy found unexpected dividends as she began to adopt the reflective listening approach we're describing: a stance of "not-being-so-sure," of noticing what she thinks or assumes about the other person and then looking again. For example, at her office Christmas party, she spent a few minutes with the husband of a co-worker about whom she'd already formed some judgment. Her co-worker was lively, but the husband had always seemed dull and withdrawn, a dud. This night, instead of doing her usual quick-and-dismissive greeting, Nancy stayed curious, asked more questions, and really paid attention to the answers. Not only was she surprised to find that the husband shared her interest in hard rock, but discovered a side to him that was animated and interesting.

"I'm really enjoying this," Nancy reports. "In the typical back-and-forth kind of conversation, I tend to get distracted, to be done after a certain time and check out. Being consciously curious helps me to stay engaged."

All the Office Is a Stage

Public speaking is another form of selling—the presenter is selling ideas (or himself). The secret shared by all great speakers is to be *un*selfconscious, to get our egos out of the way, to give priority to the audience's perspective.

As the comedian Jerry Seinfeld has noted, research shows that public speaking ranks #1 among common fears; #2 is death. Which means, as Seinfeld sardonically observes, at a funeral the person delivering the eulogy would rather be lying in the coffin.

The root of such fear is self-consciousness. How do I sound? What if I forget what I was going to say? What if I mispronounce a word? Will they think I'm stupid? Once again, innocently, we're putting the emphasis on the wrong pronoun—focusing on *I*—disconnecting, isolating us from our audience. Ever notice when the speaker loses touch that the audience begins to get restless; shifting in their seats, coughing, checking their watches? Those symptoms point toward a speaker who is detached from his listeners. His mood, his state of mind, is isolated. He has failed to sustain connection to his audience.

Public Speaking on the High Wire

Conventional: Self-Conscious	Step Up: Focus on Audience
How do I look/sound?	What is the audience feeling?
What if I misspeak?	What words resonate to them?
What will they think of me?	What are their interests and concerns?
Am I getting my point across?	Are they getting what they need from me?

Extreme fear of speaking is called stage fright. Many actors say that they feel queasy before the curtain rises, but as soon as they get into the play—as soon as they drop their focus on their own, personal thoughts—the fear dissipates. The actor connects with the character; the audience connects with the actor.

Overcoming Stage Fright

Andrea was an extremely competent advertising account executive, but terrified of public speaking. One day she had to make a presentation to a group of about 20 customers, describing progress being made on a particular project. Andrea was genuinely excited about the work she'd been doing because it was achieving great results in an area in which the group was very interested. Indeed, she was so engaged that her words came smoothly.

Then, all at once, a thought crossed her mind: "Oh, my! I'm standing here speaking to 20 people! How do I look?" Andrea began to fumble and stumble over her words.

In short, as long as her focus was on sharing with others something of mutual interest, she felt no fear of speaking. As soon as that switched to thoughts about her image, Andrea lost the ability to communicate to her audience; she lost her connection.

Fast-forward to another presentation, another group of about 20 people. Instead of her normal pattern—going over her notes one more time as audience members got a cup of coffee and found their seats—Andrea introduced herself and conversed with as many individuals as she could. As a result, she felt different. When she began to present, she found herself speaking more slowly than usual. When she opened the floor to questions, she found it easier to listen to concerns—and to make appropriate responses on the spot.

"I believed we had thought of everything, but I could totally see why they raised the concerns that they did," Andrea said. "I felt myself starting to panic over all the work we'd have to do to make the changes they wanted. But they were right—and I felt confident we'd find a way to make it work.

"It didn't even feel like I was selling, " she obeserved. "More like a conversation among friends."

Good speakers emphasize connection from the very beginning. Bob once heard Maureen Dowd, a columnist for the *New York Times*, give a keynote speech to a group of CFOs. What a mismatch! Ms. Dowd is notably liberal; most in this audience were ultra-conservative. But she disarmed them at the outset—acknowledging political differences while pointing to a common desire (to make the work place friendlier to families), even admitting that perhaps they would find nothing relevant in what she had to say. She had them paying attention from her very first sentence.

Similarly, as we make presentations, we can begin by concentrating on even a tiny step toward connection: establish eye contact with just one person, perhaps. Gradually, we can widen our perspective to include a few more individuals, then maybe everyone sitting around the room.

Staying carefully attuned to the listeners' mood is the opposite of what many of us usually do. We are tempted to tell everything in a rush of words, a flood of PowerPoint, spinning out fact upon fact in a way that simply overwhelms our intended audience. After a few minutes the torrent becomes mind numbing. Who knows what the audience is actually hearing?

Is it better to dump a bucket of water on a houseplant all at once so that it overflows, or to mete it out a little at a time—making sure that one portion of water soaks in before we add more? Slowing down our speed of speaking can actually get more information across in less time.

High-Wire Key to Strengthening Interpersonal Relationships: Put *Them* First

We are memorable and effective in sales and meetings when others can connect with what we say, when our words—and the feeling behind them—reach past their distractions to touch their own insights. In short, our individual success depends on the strength of our relationships. It's a paradox: the more we need something from others, the more important it is to remember, "It's all about *them!*"

Leadership is more tribal than scientific,
More a weaving of relationships,
Than amassing information.

—Max DePree, Chairman Emeritus,
Herman Miller

CHAPTER 8

Teams—Working as One

Key question: Too many teams take too much time to do too
little. How can I harness collective energy effectively?

"Business as usual" wasn't cutting it for the National Cattlemen's Beef Association in 2002. Demand was out of whack with supply; cattle prices were
low, and many ranchers were struggling to stay in business.

The association was tackling the problem—encouraging American consumers to eat more beef—from every possible angle. Its marketing professionals coordinated advertising and promotions around the lifestyles of
targeted customers, public relations promulgated information about nutrition
and health, and research and technical services focused on quality and food
safety. Like the three blind men trying to describe an elephant from three
vantage points, each department was working diligently from the truth; but
none grasped "the whole truth."

In short, the industry needed a new strategy that would require collaboration among those three departments. Yet they were highly independent—each
passionately convinced that their discipline was "right." Not surprisingly, the
mood was cautious as 14 representatives of the three departments assembled
in a "strategy working group" to tackle the overarching issues. Indeed, some
joked that perhaps they should set up a security checkpoint at the meeting
room door.

Four months later, that feeling had changed. The core team was able to
introduce to their 40 colleagues a new direction, focusing on previously

---

The DNA of Teams

Respect—appreciation or esteem; treating others as we wish to be treated ourselves
Integrity—saying what you mean and doing what you say
Trustworthiness—knowing that we will never deliberately do harm to others
Service—helping others achieve and grow

---

untargeted consumers with a communications strategy that addressed health concerns previously deemed intractable, and requiring new initiatives from each discipline. The group gained enthusiastic support not just because their recommendations embodied thinking that no single department could have done on its own. It was obvious that collaboration was *real* by the way core team members treated each other during their presentation, backing up each other, regardless of "department of origin." An A/V glitch that happened while a public relations pro was speaking was fixed by someone from research; a question typically in the purview of research was fielded by marketing; a challenge to promotions was answered by public relations.

In short, this team gelled. Somehow, they transcended divergent assumptions and began to work together, accomplishing far more than any one or even a subset could have done separately.

Have you, too, experienced such a team? Remember the feeling: how deeply satisfying the result, but, as important, how inspiring, even touching, the shared memories.

Of course, we'd like every team experience to be like this. In practice, however, that happens apparently at random—and all too rarely. But what if you could replicate successful teams consistently? With any type of team—work group, project, "virtual," task force, executive committee—certain aspects of human functioning must be explicitly managed. To solidify the group, the manager must think through five basic building blocks. First, ensure clarity about the common purpose: why was this team formed in the first place? Then, define measurable performance goals. For example, the purpose of the New York Yankees is to win the World Series (every year); their performance goals are winning the divisional pennant and then the Series itself. The athletes' clear understanding of the purpose and measurement is obvious in almost every interview.

The other three building blocks of teams help each person to place his or her individual talents in service of the group. The collaborative approach must specifically define:

How team members will do the work

How they will manage interpersonal dynamics

How they will hold themselves mutually accountable

The last element—mutual accountability—is where most teams struggle. The core issue, as we've discussed in chapters 6 and 7, is that we forget that our thoughts are creating separate realities. We rarely examine our ideas and assumptions. They are completely obvious to us; why are others stubbornly refusing to see things our way?

High-Wire Teams

Conventional: Force Fit	Step Up: Graceful Effectiveness
Unilateral decisions	Robust dialogues—early and often–continually re-adjust the course
Resources pre-set	Allocations respond to requests from those doing the work
Participants miss feeling of personal accomplishment	Each team member values his share in outcomes
Using power	*Unleashing power*
. . . to control the behavior of others	. . . to allow people to express their talents in ways that complement one another, and further the larger purpose
Defining freedom	*Fostering freedom*
. . . to pursue individual happiness or goals	. . . to choose to use our own creativity in shaping a role that works in concert with others

Avoiding Team Pitfalls

So, how did the beef strategy team avoid the usual pitfalls?

First, they came to the table with some shared values. Everyone was deeply dedicated to the mission and vision of the organization. And the three co-leaders knew that the challenge was too big for any department to tackle alone. Failure to coordinate efforts would result in redundancy and wasted resources; even worse, lack of collaboration would have them bumping into each other and disseminating slightly different messages to potential customers. Confusion would spawn resentment—by colleagues and by customers—and that would make things even worse.

The three co-leaders set the tone. Each was a master of his own domain and a virtual archetype of his discipline. The head of marketing was high-energy, quick to act; of public relations, soft-spoken and protective of credibility; of research, detail-oriented and careful. Yet despite their very different styles, all demonstrated respect for each other's capabilities.

Next, rather than trying to force consensus too quickly, the group "hung out in the question." In the process of probing available data, team members were assigned pieces that forced them to look at the situation—what could be done to improve the market for beef—from the perspective of a department not their own. They had to step out of their daily roles and to become advocates for "the other side" as they reflected on key issues and possible ways to address them. In conversing about "what" and "how" questions, various feelings surfaced. As participants shared their feelings, they saw their own deeply held assumptions.

During each of three meetings, one or two pieces of the puzzle were addressed. Shared discovery was fostered. Team members were continually encouraged to look for surprises, to challenge their normal way of looking at things. When discussion began to drag, the matter was tabled to the next meeting. For example, at the first meeting, the group talked about switching to a different target audience. Strong feelings surfaced on each side of the issue; people began to feel pressured, and dialogue began to devolve into debate. When the facilitator explained that no decision was necessary that day, that they were simply taking the discussion one lap around the track, the feeling lightened. The group moved on to other matters, leaving the issue of target audience to simmer on the back burner. When they reconvened for the next session a couple of weeks later, the most important targeting factors stood out, and the decision seemed natural.

In other words, the process balanced active consideration and reflection. This allowed consensus to emerge in an evolving way that didn't suck out energy. It would have been so easy—and so common—to let the urgency of the problem spur anxiety. When outcomes look big, they seem to demand quick solutions. But too many teams start with a huge flurry of activity, only to wear themselves out. When people are calm, they build sustainable momentum. That power of using the right frame of mind to accomplish collective work was demonstrated by the Cattlemen's strategy team.

Thus, even though this task added meetings to already "slammed" schedules, the participants were full of enthusiasm and vigor as they rolled out their work. As a result, the organization was well positioned to take maximum advantage of the low-carb diet craze that hit the headlines shortly thereafter—propelling fast increases in demand during the ensuing couple of years.

Teams: Undertow or Perfect Waves?

In our networked age, companies increasingly rely on teams as their orga-nizing construct. Indeed, teamwork promises productivity and a supportive work life. The benefits of teamwork may be most obvious when times are toughest, and the organization has nowhere to go but up. In a turnaround or in a climb to market leadership, the sense of accomplishment can be joyous; the friendships that develop can last a lifetime.

"I think of teams like perfect waves breaking against a sandy beach," says a former colleague. "They form some distance out, curl into a graceful peak, seem to hang momentarily in midair, then crash against the shore and dissipate." Ah, yes! That is the nature of teams—shaping human energy to create something beautiful and then ending when their purpose is complete.

But often we experience teamwork as mere drudgery. The manager spouts "all for one" mantras and then makes decisions unilaterally. It's hard to get anything done because the functional leaders resist team recommenda-tions and give resources grudgingly. Or certain individuals bear the brunt of responsibility, while others coast. Too many teams seem to take time away from our real jobs, and obscure our individual accomplishments.[1]

What if these frustrations were less the fault of the team concept than a shortcoming in understanding how successful teams work?

The Essential Power of Connection

For too long we've followed a model that says that accomplishment depends on leaders who are lionhearted heroes. Independence is so deeply valued, particularly in the United States, that peers often keep their distance from one another. But people are getting tired of playing this game. The young adults we see entering the job force value affinity (which we define as warm under-standing that makes clear our powerful connection to others, releasing wisdom and rekindling energy with a synergistic intelligence).[2]

Loving Her Job

Kate, a newly minted Tulane graduate, selected her first job intuitively, based on the feeling of the workplace. A highly sought-after candidate, she narrowed her choice to two retail companies—archrivals with prestigious reputations. But the feeling at the two firms could not have been more different. Kate ultimately chose to go where the staff was having more fun. She noticed that people said hello in the hallways, referred to small celebratory events, and genuinely seemed

> to like each other. She just loves her job, finds it fascinating. Above all, Kate feels she is learning tons as co-workers actually take the time to help her learn the art of buying and the mechanics of planning.
>
> Her classmate went to the rival, and six months into the job hated it. "Kate, most people abhor working here. They think of themselves as being better than anyone else, and that arrogance seeps into everything we do."

In other words, work is, in effect, spiritual—another word, like faith, avoided in the business context. The word seems so, well, soft and New Age, but it is actually utilitarian. It describes how we connect to transcendent intelligence and to each other.

"Even for those who don't consider themselves 'spiritual' in a conventional sense, creating a successful team—whether it's an NBA champion or a record-setting sales force—is essentially a spiritual act," writes Phil Jackson, who coached the Chicago Bulls to six NBA championships in the 1990s, and then coached the LA Lakers to three more. "It requires the individuals involved to surrender their self-interest for the greater good so that the whole adds up to more than the sum of its parts."[3]

Higher Levels of Team Accomplishment

What often sinks teams is failure to surpass the limits of individual imaginations. Members spend most of their time immersed in self-centered concerns. They brood over such questions as: "What if my contribution isn't recognized?" or "How come I always get stuck with the hardest jobs?" or even "I have the best answer so why doesn't the team just do it my way?" Such thoughts aren't bad in themselves. But our desperate need to keep the focus on *me* distances us from others. It ultimately diminishes our own effectiveness, as well as that of the team.

What can loosen ego's grip on team behavior? Remember that each person is shaping a reality based on their individual thoughts, and those thoughts are ephemeral. That awareness may clear our minds. What seemed so vital, so life-and-death important, suddenly seems insignificant or even humorous. New possibilities become clear.

As we've seen in chapter 6, the #1 job for a team leader is to monitor the group's tone, its mood. Using optimum mental acuity requires clear-headedness. Listening to others requires freedom from the distractions of worried or anxious thoughts. So the manager must check in with her own emotions from time to time, as well as monitor the emotions in the room.

When the members of a team begin functioning with a higher state of clarity, they can achieve new levels of accomplishment—and do so with graceful effectiveness. Because their thinking is composed, they are able to see things from a broad perspective, overcome obstacles quickly, and anticipate problems before they arise. Participants stay on task without reacting to disruptive thoughts, so meetings become stimulating ways to get things done. Even the most difficult issues do not upset team members, who know that a clear mental state will enable them to discover solutions. Ultimately, everyone begins to show leadership, accessing Mother Wit and contributing unique skill when it is called for.

Look again at the Chicago Bulls. Michael Jordan, arguably the greatest player in the history of basketball, was the centerpiece of the team when Phil Jackson came onboard in 1987. "The conventional wisdom is that the team was primarily a one-man show—Michael Jordan and the Jordanaires," Jackson notes. But it wasn't until Jackson moved Jordan and the team to "the power of *oneness*," of "*we versus me*," that the championship string began, broken only after Jordan retired (for the first time) in 1993.

On Jordan's return in 1995, another championship was assumed to be in the bag. "But what happened instead was that the team lost the close identity it had forged in Jordan's absence and regressed to the way it had been in the late eighties," writes Jackson, "when the players were so mesmerized by his moves that they played as if they were mere spectators at the show."[4]

The High-Wire Shift in Team Thinking

Conventional: 'Lip Service'	Step Up: Genuine Connection
"I'm the only one who gets it"	Trust in others' common sense
Resent distraction from "real job"	Appreciate larger purpose
Disrupt meetings	Stimulate conversations centered on the task
Fret over every glitch	Sustain confidence that solutions will be found for even the most complex issues
Chafe in harness	Open to affinity for others
Vie for personal recognition, rewards	Share in abundance: plenty of "good stuff" to go around

How Incentives May Actually Undercut Teams

Encouraging the focus on *me*, well-intentioned incentive programs can actually hinder team performance. To motivate workers, we reward "the A-team" with bonuses; "the weakest links" get, when worse comes to worst, severance packages. When our company needs to develop a new product, we create a contest,

Bob's 14-year-old son Remy was helping his dad rent a car at the Tampa airport when he noticed the "Employee of the Month" award on the wall. "Hey, Dad! That's not fair!" Remy blurted out. "What about everyone else; didn't they do a good job, too?" The agent was so touched that she gave them a two-class upgrade and let Remy pick out the car.

pitting teams against each other; whichever comes up with the best idea gets a prize. To prove we're "best in class," we submit projects for industry awards; the employee or team that brings home such glory gets a bonus. In our own careers, the perks for personal performance have ranged from the usual—tickets to the movies; attendance at an off-site with choice of golf, tennis, or a day at the spa—to the imaginative—a case of Taittinger champagne; a seat on a professional tour to Asia, Australia, and Tahiti.

And what's wrong with that? Incentive theory goes all the way back to amoebas in the lab. Poke an amoeba with something unpleasant and it will shrink away. Put sugar nearby, and it will move toward the reward.

But, presumably unlike amoebas, we are thinking creatures. Incentives, however sweet, stimulate our imaginations. What's going to be required next? Will I continue to be good enough to get my reward? Am I getting as much as the amoeba in the office next door?

And why single out one person's conduct when a team is required to give the customer a satisfactory experience? The problem with typical incentives is that they imply competition; there's only so much good stuff to go around, and I need to elbow others aside (or even sabotage them) to make sure I get my share. Spurning such temptation can be tremendously powerful, as demonstrated by the cast of *Friends*. Early in the show's run, David Schwimmer was in a position to command star treatment. Instead, he went to the other five members of the ensemble cast and got them to negotiate their contracts as a unit: whatever one would get, all would get. That team of actors attributed the show's long run at the top of the ratings to the strong bonds and creative collaboration engendered by Schwimmer's unselfish foresight.

But that's not typical in corporate America. Our usual team metaphors come from sports—blocking and tackling, driving toward the goal line, hitting a home run—in which individual records are celebrated.

What would an organization feel like if reference points came, instead, from music? For example, Tom Watson dubbed confabs of leaders from various agencies of Omnicom, the giant advertising conglomerate, "Jazz Meetings." The metaphor was apt, Watson felt, because within jazz combos each player

"We versus Me"

The misuse of teams is so prevalent, and so costly, that we feel compelled to restate the obvious: there is no real separation between any of us, *except in our thoughts*. Turn down the volume on *your own* internal dialogue; become genuinely curious about the *others'* perspectives.

improvises from her own creativity yet with awareness of the others. Each has a time to solo, and a time to harmonize or to support. The result is interplay of notes and rhythms—in other words, beautiful music.

Conversely, the most insidious, overlooked danger of competition is that it encourages comparisons. As we strive to "get mine," we constantly look over our shoulders—are "they" gaining on us? Inevitably, however, comparison turns inward; possibly without even being aware, I begin to judge my own performance, as well as that of others. Someone else would do it better; I could do better; I'm not as good as I used to be—or as I should be.

The more we judge ourselves in comparison to others or to some unrealistic standard, the more insecure we become. As we saw in chapter 2, the greater the insecurity, the less mental energy we have available. On and on, negative comparison erodes productivity. Competitive criticisms—of our teammates and ultimately of ourselves—drain our energy. We divert the resources we could bring to bear on the challenges in front of us.

High-Wire Key to Harnessing Collective Energy: Make Work a Dance

No doubt the manager needs to be clear about focusing goals, smart about how work is structured, intelligent about who performs which role, and lucid about the assumptions governing strategy. But these tangible components of effective teamwork can take hold only when the manager ensures that team members are feeling connected and appreciative toward each other.

To get a deeper sense of this kind of collaboration, watch a tango. The man's job is to lead, providing firm direction by the pressure of his hand and the bend of his body. The woman's is equally important: to follow, yielding resistance without becoming passive. The effort becomes art rather than exercise when the movement flows without conscious thought. Each partner senses the intent of the other in an intricate but seamless pattern. Each individual's style disappears; the pair works as one.

When we work as one, we lose our own ego in the dance. Thereby we achieve something transformational—even if it endures only until the music stops, the championship is won, or the job is completed.

> Now this is the Law of the Jungle–
> As old and true as the sky;
> And the wolf that shall keep it may prosper,
> But the wolf that shall break it must die.
> As the creeper that girdles the tree trunk,
>   The Law runneth forward and back–
> For the strength of the Pack is the Wolf,
> And the strength of the Wolf is the Pack.
>
> —Rudyard Kipling

CHAPTER 9

Managing Conflict

Key question: How can I accommodate conflicts so that they energize my staff, rather than provoking resistance and resentment?

John was shouting at his colleague, Mark, across the dinner table. He was speaking so loudly that he was literally spitting words out of his mouth. Mark hunkered down, seething internally but not saying much. Then he exploded, calling John all kinds of names. Bill, their manager, happened to walk into the restaurant at the height of the shouting match. He realized that two exceptionally talented people, going at each other this hard—and in front of three co-workers—was sure to cause lasting damage. What would you do if you had been their manager?

Overcoming the impulse to join the mêlée (or turn on his heel), Bill approached the table and said, "Why don't we all take a ten-minute timeout" and sat down. He said nothing. In reaction, the two protagonists said nothing; the co-workers said nothing. For fully ten minutes Bill just sat, not saying anything, silently calling to mind how much he enjoyed working with John and Mark, appreciating how talented they were, and how glad he was that they were part of the company.

Bill's demeanor had a calming effect on everyone. Then one of the observers chuckled softly and said, "Wow, that reminded me of watching a summer thunderstorm coming across Lake Michigan. Raging violence, noise, rain, wind, and a couple of hailstones for good measure—followed by an indelible tranquility that is just so beautifully peaceful."

John turned to Mark and apologized, and Mark responded in kind. Then John matter-of-factly put his issue on the table and said, "Look, I was taking myself way too seriously because I really thought that my answer was the only way; but let's take a step back and see if we can talk through our differences. Is that OK with you, Mark?" "Sure," Mark replied.

Within minutes they not only had resolved their conflict but also had come up with a way to handle a whole category of similar issues that became standard company practice.

Later that evening John sat with Bill in the lobby of their hotel and thanked him. "When I saw you walking up to our table, I thought you were going to take my head off. I was all set to tell you why I was right and Mark was wrong," he said. "But after a few minutes of not saying anything at all, I realized that maybe I didn't have all the answers, and that helped me regain my mental balance."

Expect Conflict

Like John and Mark, each of us works from different assumptions and beliefs. "Facts" are filtered through the lens of our individual thoughts. For example, when viewing financial results, "Is the glass half full or half empty?" The same set of "facts" can provoke wildly divergent views of how the business is performing, depending on how two people choose to interpret the numbers.

In short, conflict is inescapable because we think for ourselves. While institutions are invented to harness collective energy, each person in them is shaping his own *reality* from personal, moment-to-moment thoughts. As a result, management often feels it's like herding cats. You point toward a goal, but your colleagues pursue their individual interests based on how the world looks to them.

A classic exercise illustrates the point. A "crime" is staged in front of a group, and each "eyewitness" is asked what happened. The testimonies inevitably vary, in details large and small. That's because our thinking causes each of us to emphasize certain things and to ignore others, to fill in gaps and to paint our own mental picture of what is *real*. Yet we assume that we are seeing the whole picture—the truth, the whole truth, and nothing but the truth.

When we feel compelled to defend our reality, judging any other interpretation as flat-out wrong, we engender conflicts that can go on and on. People choose sides; positions become entrenched; and, finally, "winners and losers" emerge. But when so much effort has been diverted to internal conflict, the real winners are likely to be the company's competitors!

Given that conflict is inescapable, it's futile to try to eliminate it. As a matter of fact, some bosses believe that they can actually use conflict to spur employees to perform—setting one against the other as shown in the hit TV show, *The Apprentice.* But that kind of management breeds insecurity, which undermines good decision making and long-term performance.

So is there a way to deal with differences that helps, rather than hinders, achievement?

Friction at Work

At the Space Camp operated by NASA in Huntsville, Alabama, the positive side of friction is demonstrated vividly. Campers strap on astronaut shoes and go into a replica of the Space Lab. There, they are asked to walk across a floor perforated by tiny holes. With air streaming through, the coefficient of friction is very, very low, simulating a low-gravity environment. Try as they might, campers find it impossible to walk across that floor. The Space Campers see that friction isn't simply a drag, something that slows down progress or causes waste. Friction helps to achieve locomotion. Countless other useful applications of friction are all around us.

So, although we don't want to encourage friction (i.e., conflict) among co-workers, neither do we need to fear it. The important question is: how can we attain worthwhile ends from the differences that arise in the pursuit of any collective activity? In other words, how can we achieve resolution that strengthens group commitment to move forward in a way that benefits our joint endeavors?

The answer at many institutions is a hierarchical norm. A senior executive resolves conflict by fiat, using the power of his position. You know the drill: the troops fight it out until the leader intervenes and tells people the way it will be. This lowers the decibel level so that the manager may believe everything is settled once and for all.

But often it merely drives the issue underground, causing problems behind the scenes. For one thing, the losers do not go away but live to fight another day, often by resisting implementation. The harder the leader pushes, the more the dissenters dig in their heels. Even more important: when employees are "just following orders," they make no personal investment in the outcome. They feel neither accountable, nor responsible (as discussed in chapter 5).

High-Wire Conflict Resolution

Conventional: Compromise	Step Up: Consensus
"What was he thinking?"	"What was *he* thinking?
Avoid the heart of disagreements	Probe points of view; calmly assess what others *really* care about
Unquestioning loyalty admired	Common sense encouraged
Goals are dictated and fixed	Goals and context are part of the discussion
Debate the details	Build from shared values
Keeping score: who's giving, and giving up, more	Keeping faith: eye on the ultimate prize
Everybody somewhat dissatisfied-even if equally so	Teams motivated to work
Little real change	Breakthrough innovations

Why Compromises Fail

A second way to resolve conflicts is our old democratic friend, majority rule. For people who are accustomed to working in hierarchies, majority rule has powerful appeal. But it actually has the same flaw as top-down management: built-in resistance. Again, it doesn't really resolve disagreements; rather, they go undercover. The initial conflict will surface again and again as the minority seeks to recover what they lost in the voting process.

In addition, it is too easy for majority rule to result in bureaucracy that takes the wind out of the sails of innovation. Endless procedures govern the process, all in the name of ensuring fairness. Ultimately, people are turned off because it takes too much effort to resolve even the simplest questions. In one extreme case, we found a company that had memo letterhead permanently engraved with the words "circulating for nonobjection"!

The handmaiden of majority rule is compromise: you give up a little of what you want, and I give up a little of what I want; we accept something in the middle. We both swallow a bit of unhappiness. "Satisficing," as stated by Herbert Simon, the economist who pioneered the field of "bounded rationality," means that we end up with something we agree not to fight over, but that motivates neither of us.[1] More than that, we make an entry in our mental accounts: "I gave up 'y' this time, so you owe me 'x' next time."

But, by its very nature, conflict often is the doorway to tremendous opportunity. At its core, conflict is merely about the clashing of at least two different thought habits—different assumptions or beliefs that can be so deeply rooted that we long ago stopped examining their relevance. Strong feelings about an issue are a signal that maybe the time has come to set aside old beliefs and look for new insights.

In other words, conflict can force us to think of different ways to reach our goals, or of different goals altogether. All we need is to be willing to examine *what we don't know* instead of clinging stubbornly to what we think we already understand. In short, instead of settling for compromise, invest the time and energy necessary for consensus.

In Search of the Common Denominator

The four partners were divided over a firm's strategy. Should they branch into a new area, or stick to their knitting? For a full 18 months the topic was discussed in meetings, dinners, even hallway conversations. As the staff took sides, profits began to suffer.

At an off-site, the partners happened to sit together at lunch. Relaxing as they looked over a beautiful beach, they recounted stories about the early days. Remembering shared adversity and triumphs, they recaptured warm feelings for each other. Then someone brought up the ongoing conflict. "If a client were trying to find a way through an impasse like ours, what would we advise him to do?"

Good question—one that opened the way to an answer not clouded by personal ego or emotion. Shifting focus from the two proposed—and polarized—courses of action, they realized that all agreed that their core business was maturing, and they needed "a second act." They had to develop new service lines—whether to attract a new set of clients or to deepen relationships with the current core businesses.

That common denominator provided a rallying point. Within a day, the firm outlined a strategy. The partners and staff left the off-site energized to face the challenge ahead.

The Seed of Genius: Consensus

Consider two people sitting in a library. One person wants to open the window for some cool air; the other wants to keep the window shut to reduce street noise. Seemingly an intractable conflict—until they discover that by opening the window in an adjacent room, both of their desires can be fulfilled. They can achieve consensus.

One place to learn about the power of consensus in conflict resolution is jury duty. Betsy sat with 11 strangers one long afternoon, deliberating whether an attractive blonde was guilty of driving under the influence of alcohol. The young woman had testified that she had skipped lunch and dinner, had "just two glasses of wine" at a party, which she left shortly after midnight. She was

---

From Jury Room to Office

Lessons of Collaboration

- Replace fear of conflict with faith in everyone's ability to put aside personal agendas ("what outcome serves me") in service to a larger purpose
- Take lightly what you already think — pay it less attention — so that you may truly understand what others are saying
- Invest time in shared discovery, which encourages unity

---

following her boyfriend's car on the way to an all-night diner when a police officer pulled her over. Results from a field sobriety test were problematic; a Breathalyzer test, taken at the station 30 minutes later, measured her blood alcohol at just over the legal limit.

The jury was in conflict. Some members believed that the defendant hadn't drunk enough wine to be impaired. Haven't we all had two glasses of wine at a party, and didn't we feel in control behind the wheel as we drove home? Others felt the Breathalyzer result was somewhat "iffy." And a few were convinced that the defendant must have drunk more wine than she'd testified to.

After four hours, it seemed that the jury would be hung. In one last effort to avoid a mistrial, they reviewed the testimony of an expert brought in by the defense to explain how the body processes alcohol. The expert assumed that the defendant had drunk two glasses of wine between 11:00 P.M. and midnight. Therefore, he explained, the amount of alcohol in her bloodstream would have been just below the legal limit at the time the police officer stopped her. But the body would have continued to absorb more alcohol, explaining a higher-than-legal reading at the station later.

The jurors took a different approach. Instead of starting with an assumed two glasses of wine and *looking forward,* they started with the Breathalyzer reading at 1 A.M. and *moved backward.* Plotting data on a blackboard, they saw that the defendant *must* have already been over the limit when she was driving and actually must have drunk more wine than she had admitted.

In other words, the panel invested the time to make a shared discovery. That experience galvanized everyone in the room. It opened mental doorways to fresh thoughts that resolved the differences. A verdict became obvious: guilty. The process of *together* setting aside what we "know must be true" and looking instead at "what we don't know" is one effective way of seeing a deeper truth that resolves discord.

Human Connection—A Necessary Requirement for Conflict Resolution

One caution—no resolution or fresh learning will take place if emotions dominate. When conflict escalates to bad feelings, a stalemate ensues. Our thoughts grip us so tightly that we won't budge, much less look for something new. Nope! Mental turmoil can quickly turn to remembering all kinds of good reasons why we are right and the other person is wrong. Memory, fueled by passion, cements justification.

That's why managers who are able to sustain goodwill toward others resolve conflicts gracefully. Even though they may feel a strong emotion during the conversation, that doesn't stop them from truly seeing another person operating just as they are. Indeed, we are all trying to do the best we can, given the thoughts that occur to us moment-to-moment.

When Fury Has Run Its Course

"No decision should take more than 30 minutes," announced the facilitator of a meeting at Exult. The executive team was considering immediate decisions that would significantly influence the business' long-run success. Aware of how high the stakes were, yet rushing to work within the imposed time constraint, the group got into one ferocious argument after another.

Eventually, the fury ran its course, and inquisitiveness crept into the conversation. At that point it became apparent that the fight stemmed from nothing more than differing interpretations of what "now" meant! To the head of operations, "now" meant action "X" had to happen in the next 30 to 60 days. To the CEO, "now" meant over the next 12 to 18 months. Their argument had less to do with the right course of action and everything to do with each person's assumptions about time frames.

High-Wire Key to Handling Conflicts: Keep Your Own Bearings

It's a cinch that we'll be more effective in every business situation if we slow down our thinking enough to recognize the different perspectives of the people with whom we are engaged. Resolving conflicts looks difficult because it appears that the only way to achieve it is by imposing a new order on others. But what if we probe the issue of conflicts with a different question: *How do we manage to get along at all?*

Actually, we have more in common than we realize. While the content of our thinking differs, each of us is the same in the *fact that we think*. We are all caught up in our own thoughts. We are all doing the best we can even when we forget that we are the thinkers and take our thoughts too seriously. So, in a sense, we are all innocent sufferers of the same delusional force. And each of us enjoys the same possibility: at any moment we can drop the veil that prevents our seeing that we are the source of our thoughts. In that instant, we find it hard to keep investing so much mental energy in whatever line of thinking we are having.

For example, when Matt was a freshman at the University of California at Berkeley, a woman in his dorm suffered a panic attack. No one could calm her down but Matt. How did he do it? "First I agreed with her," he explained. In other words, he established a connection by acknowledging that her fearful thoughts were creating her reality—they looked real to her and so she was acting on them. Matt wasn't being fake; he respected the fact that his dorm-mate's thoughts were exerting a powerful grip on her behavior at that moment.

When we experience someone "losing it," we may find it hard to maintain our own mental tranquility—just as it can be hard to keep our bearings during a fierce argument. But once we are aware of the nature of thought, we realize that conflict simply spotlights the particular thought patterns in which each person is stuck. As Bill showed in the example at the start of this chapter, the manager's job in confronting conflict is *not* to supply another viewpoint or answer. It is to keep calm and cool *himself*—knowing that his feelings can change the emotional tone. And once the tone has improved, the protagonists will be able to find their own resolution.

Compromise does not create,
It deals with what already exists.

　　　　　—Mary Parker Follett[2]

CHAPTER 10

Employee Relations

Key question: How do I handle difficult conversations and performance problems—saying what needs to be said without making things go from bad to worse?

Tanya was a newly minted HR manager for a major insurance company. She called Bob because she was worried about an upcoming meeting with a departmental employee, Pete. He was very disruptive: coming into work late, missing assignments, being rude to co-workers, all while producing the best work of anyone in the section—when he chose to get down to the task at hand. That high-quality output was delivered at a cost to nearly everyone around Pete, earning him the private nickname "Mr. Trouble." Nevertheless, Pete enjoyed a privileged position with the boss, who was too distant to see Pete's negative impact on staff morale, but was impressed by his terrific output.

Tanya knew that everyone on her new team was intently watching her management skill—that a confrontation with Pete could make or break her reputation, and she would be living with that consequence for a long time to come. So Bob could hear the tenseness in her voice when he took her call.

As she poured out the story, Tanya spiraled into worry; she had no idea how to fix Mr. Trouble's behavior. She felt that the only way to keep her stature as a manager was to fire him—an outcome that was sure to cost her with the boss.

Bob could have outlined strategies for handling disruptive employees. He might have suggested such tactics as proactive listening, constructive feedback, even the legal steps necessary for termination. Instead, Bob began with a simple question: "Tanya, it seems like you are letting your fear and imagination have a party in your head. What would it take for you to stop feeding that mental chatter and just be present with me, right now?"

The phone grew silent.

And then Tanya laughed—a rich, resonant laugh from the soul. "Thanks," she said, "I remember now that quiet space in my mind which feels so good. I guess I can find a way to resolve this problem if I just remember that all of us, including Mr. Trouble, have the ability to find their common sense when their mind is calm."

Bob ran into Tanya several weeks later and asked what had happened. She said, "You know, it was really surprising. Pete came into my office very agitated; I could tell that his mind was racing. So I sat quietly, offered him a cup of coffee, which I got myself. Both of us just sat sipping our drinks. And in a few minutes I could feel him relax as we connected. I guess he may have been afraid, too. So then it occurred to me to ask him if he was happy at work. He said no, that he hated coming through the front door every morning even though he loved the sense of accomplishment from the assignments. That provoked my curiosity, so I asked him why.

"What he said blew me away—'I hate being around people!' From that point it took us only a few minutes to conclude that the best option was for him to work from home, something I could agree to if he became an independent contractor. The whole thing took just 30 minutes, and everyone was pleased. Best of all, Pete has been doing even better work since he started working from home and feeling less pressure."

High-Wire Employee Relations

Conventional: Intensive Process	Step Up: Resilient Resolution
Avoid confrontation as long as possible	Engage in early dialogue
"Paper trail" deviations from expectations	Probe for insecurity
Reprimand/punish	Seek agreement on new possibilities
If necessary, termination handled by HR/legal	If necessary, separation from the company leaves all—employee, manager, co-workers—reconciled to an obvious outcome

Ending the Game of Avoidance

Nonperformance, noncompliance, rudeness, lack of integrity or trust, skill shortfalls, and poor work habits are examples of ways that employees can bother colleagues and employers. Co-workers complain, customers are treated rudely, managers are ignored. Yet a normal assumption is that the best outcome we can hope for is that the situation will resolve itself.

Many managers dance in tortured avoidance, trying to sidestep conflict. Too often, behaviors are not addressed until things have deteriorated beyond redemption. Or the fix is left to the HR staff, usually by following procedures that result in dismissal. Not only is this an intensive process that wastes time for both managers and HR staff, it can also create bitter feelings on the part of a former employee. Worst of all, it can weaken confidence among other team members.

It doesn't have to be that way. For example, the management of St. John's Hospital in Jackson Hole, Wyoming, has perfected a tough-minded but warm-hearted way of addressing employee performance questions. It disseminates a short list of guidelines:

- Maintain a feeling of respect
- Listen with an open mind (not making assumptions or jumping to conclusions)
- Be willing to admit mistakes on the management side
- Explore the issue, seeking outcomes that work for all parties, the patients, and the hospital
- Ensure that the performance expectation is understood by both parties

Managers at all levels are taught from their first day on the job to engage in such conversations as soon as they hear about a problem. How are these skills taught?

Lead administrators model the defined behaviors with powerful teaching impact. When executives hold one another accountable for actively using the guidelines, that accountability is felt systemwide.

And St. John's leaders solicit feedback about the guidelines' relevance and usefulness. More than any teaching device, such openness ensures that everyone knows that these are not mere slogans on the wall. It shows by the walk, not the talk, that people will be treated fairly.

In addition, the HR professionals see that teaching the skills of handling performance problems is an essential part of their job. So instead of cleaning up employee relations issues after the damage has been done, they intervene at the first sign of trouble. That intervention is directed at the manager or supervisor—with the goal of preparing him or her to engage the employee in a calm conversation.[1]

Questions to Ask before Reprimands

- Do we both understand what thinking might have caused him/her to behave in that way?
- Have I assumed that he/she knew, believed, or understood something that actually hadn't been made clear?
- How much of my own insecure thinking (concern about how my subordinate's actions reflect on me) has been triggered?
- Can I share my observations in a neutral, exploratory way?

What St. John's leaders have learned is that the first step in better employee relations is to adopt a different perspective, to cut the subject down to size. Typically, the disruptive employee is spewing out emotion as a cover-up or protection for some sort of underlying insecurity. Think of him like a bully— all threat on the outside, but often a scared kid within. Or like the Wizard of Oz—projecting an imposing bluster, while a very ordinary person punches buttons and insists, "Pay no attention to that man behind the curtain."

Employee issues, like all disagreements, are shaped by everyone's ability to create her unique *reality* from her own thoughts. If an employee thinks she is doing everything well, the manager can't simply provide a list of changes required. What looks like tangible evidence of poor performance to the manager is likely to provoke counterclaims listing results or protests citing the unfairness of the standards by which the employee is being judged— all supported by her personal view.

A typical example played out at one company that wanted to ease conversations about promotions. With the best of intentions, the HR department identified 13 performance factors, and then described elements of each one at every level of the organization chart. But the list got so long that hopeful employees could not prioritize. They could not distinguish between satisfying basic job requirements, such as meeting deadlines, and above-and-beyond-the-call "promotable" achievement, such as innovating new programs. They would count how many boxes they had checked off, rather than weighing what it really took to succeed at the next level—the two or three key factors separating one position from the next. So any promotion denied led to an intractable confrontation.

The Fault Lies Partly in Ourselves

Instead of detailed content, the path to resolving even the nastiest employee issue is listening with rapport. In chapters 6 and 7, we discussed rapport as an essential component, and showed its use in more effective sales calls and meetings. When it comes to performance issues, often the heart of the problem is egocentric thinking, which is manifested in self-centered behavior.

Are We Even in the Same Time Zone?

> Tracy had a couple of years' experience at a small company but accepted an entry-level position at a larger firm. Standard operating procedure dictated that after a year, entry-level employees were evaluated and either promoted or encouraged to seek other career options. But Tracy felt her prior experience should weigh in the balance.
>
> Six months into her first year, Tracy went to her supervisor and said, "I've been doing great work; when will I be promoted?" The supervisor answered, "Soon." The following Tuesday, Tracy was back again. The problem: for the supervisor, a 20-year veteran, "soon" was six months or more. For Tracy, six months equaled a quarter of her career—and her manager's "soon" left Tracy unsatisfied.

In high-wire employee relations, the manager seeks to create feelings of warmth, care, and compassion so that individuals on both sides can step back from their personal thinking and see a bigger picture.

The place to begin is in *our own* thinking about the situation. Are we really dealing with a difficult employee—our own Mr. Trouble? Or do we see a capable person who, for some reason, is exhibiting behaviors that are not in the best interests of the organization? And do we then wonder what's going on: is there some insecurity or other thinking that is throwing our colleague off-balance?

Feeling compassion for the insecurity in other people does not mean we condone bad behavior. Nor do we become a doormat. But seeing how thought leads to behavior helps us keep our own balance, and that gives us ready access to powerful responsiveness.

The road to hell in communication is paved with us/them, right/wrong interactions. When we presume malicious intent—or, at least, selfish motivation—we easily succumb to our own negative reactions. That narrows our view of solutions and resolutions. To avoid these potholes, when you catch yourself making an assumption, switch to a stance of puzzlement. "How interesting that he would say that. I wonder what he sees or feels that I'm missing?"

Respect is implicit in this process. The manager acknowledges the employee's right to experience her own reality—experience filtered through her thinking. Such respect lowers the emotional temperature for the employee and the manager; it helps both to step back from their own right answers—to be able to truly communicate.

> ## Gracefully Delivering Feedback
>
> One of GE's senior managers is renowned for his ability to give unpleasant feedback. Once he feels the tone is right—in other words, he and the employee are relating well—he asks permission to explore the performance issue. He doesn't say much, nor does he need to. He knows the key is to ask questions and then listen. When he does speak, he's most likely to share an insight that has emerged naturally as he listens.
>
> Sometimes a surprising answer arises, such as the employee resigning voluntarily. On other occasions, a remedial program is put in place; this may lead to a turnaround in problematic behaviors.
>
> Regardless of what happens, the manager's goal is to reach a dignified conclusion in an expeditious fashion.

High-Wire Key to Difficult Conversations/Performance Issues: Compassion with Rigor

Every manager confronts employee problems and must engage in difficult conversations. The key to navigating such interactions with employees is not a pat technique. There's no magic list of specific steps guaranteed to work for every person, every type of situation.

As in other aspects of management, the issue is not what we *do* but how we *are*. Again, we must rely on awareness: seeing the importance of stepping back from upset thoughts. When we choose to work from a stance grounded in compassion, in our common struggle with thinking-run-amok, even the worst employee issues can be resolved with grace.

Rigor is maintained not by harsh tone but by adherence to the gold standard: achieving results in the way that matters to others in the company. Commitment to the best outcome is what makes even warm-hearted conversations tough-minded.

It takes two to speak truth—
One to speak and one to hear.

—Henry David Thoreau

Marge, it takes two to lie—
One to talk; one to listen.

—Homer Simpson

THIRD PRECEPT

The Calmer You Become, the More Powerful You Become—and the More You Can Achieve

CHAPTER 11

Focus and Clarity

Key question: As I move from working in the trenches to framing the big picture, what thinking patterns do I need to change? And how?

"I'm in the weeds and dying there," moaned Dolores. She was an indispensable employee in a fast-growing housewares firm—the only person besides the president who had survived new ownership and restructuring. As a matter of fact, Dolores had started as the president's secretary and worked up to be product manager; she knew not only all the boss's hot buttons, but also the history of every product and of every customer relationship. All day long, she dug into her files, and her memory banks, to answer questions. "I'm 'Information Central,'" Dolores observed, with equal parts pride and frustration.

Having shown the ropes to a succession of marketing directors, Dolores yearned for promotion herself. But while she was tracking down details for other staffers, she fell farther and farther behind in her own responsibilities—particularly in making decisions regarding new product strategies. Yes, everybody relied on Dolores. But they couldn't see her making the leap to management leadership.

Dolores had bumped into what we call the Great Divide—that point on the corporate ladder where the next rung depends not on what we do ourselves, but how we mobilize the team. Not on thinking about the tactics of a specific task, but on framing the larger context necessary to focus group energy.

Indeed, in the hierarchy of management responsibilities, keeping the organization focused is second only to maintaining a positive tone (see chapter 6).

As we have said, organizations exist to accomplish work greater than what can be done by a single individual. The bigger the dream, the less important is the manager's own contribution to its realization. He must count on the ability of others to figure out what needs to be done and how best to go about doing it. And in order to bring a vision to life, the manager must help people gain *clarity.*

Driving Toward a Singular Vision

> Toyota had a dream in the late 1940s: "catching up with Ford."
> President Toyoda Kiichiro and Head of Manufacturing Taiichi Ohno
> realized that the ratio of Japanese to American automobile workers
> was 10:1. In other words, it took only ten Americans to do the work of
> 100 Japanese. Surely, Toyota's leaders thought, it couldn't be true that
> the American worker could exert ten times more physical effort than the
> Japanese, so they must be working smarter.
>
> Toyota's leaders set out to best the United States almost as a matter
> of survival. They had no idea how to go about doing it, but counted on
> the ingenuity of their workforce to eliminate waste. They initiated
> an approach that considered implementing any idea that could save even
> half a step, or the time it takes for a hand to reach out for something. The
> resulting Toyota Production System has given us such concepts as "just
> in time" flow of inventories (*kanban*) and continuous improvement
> (*kaizen*). As a result, Toyota beat the Americans at their own game and
> raised the performance bar for every automobile manufacturer.[1]

The Power of Presence

We speak of managers who inspire their teams as having great "presence." A key element in that is *actual* presence: dismissing anything that detracts from what is happening and what is needed, *in this moment.* Unwavering resolve or focus means, as they say in sports, that we "keep our head in the game."

David Pottruck, former president and CEO of the Charles Schwab Corporation, talked about presence in an interview with *Fortune*: "When I'm on the slopes, all I'm thinking is, 'Stay vertical.' At all costs, stay vertical! Seriously, I'm usually focused on sort of the challenge of the mountain. . . . You don't have time to think of the mechanics—move your foot here, point your toe here. You're thinking of the rhythm. You're in the flow. It's such a wonderful feeling. You're moving with the terrain. You can't think about anything else, or you'll fall."[2]

This feeling is described after practically every championship game, no matter what the sport. The athletes on the winning team attribute their success to being focused, "in the groove," "in the flow," or "in the zone." They say how *clear* everything seemed (figure 11.1). In other words, they've been eliminating distractions, getting priorities straight, putting extraneous things out of their minds.

Case in point: Super Bowl XXIII in 1989, in which the San Francisco 49ers came from behind in the last two minutes of the game with a 92-yard touchdown drive to beat the Cincinnati Bengals, 20-16. Later, star receiver Jerry Rice said that he had felt so focused that he heard no noise from the sell-out crowd from the first huddle of that last drive, through a series of plays down the field, until teammate John Taylor caught quarterback Joe Montana's pass in the end zone with 34 seconds left. Then, and only then, did Rice heard the roar of the crowd.

Moments like these demonstrate that accomplishment simply requires seeing the essence of the task and then doing the obvious the best you can. The task itself guides us in the most direct way to perform it. Knowing this essence is what enables all performers to access their full creative faculties and talents. It's what enables us, in the middle of delivering a PowerPoint presentation for the 22nd time, to be bowled over by fresh insights about the material or the audience. Our slides may be exactly the same. But we have become responsive in the moment, and our presentation achieves a grace that transcends our spoken words.

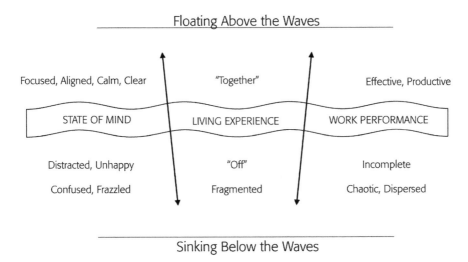

FIGURE 11.1

The clearer our state of mind, the more we feel grounded—and the more we are able to sustain the focus of our team.

Focus is not about willpower. It is the calm elimination of
distracting thoughts that unleashes productive energy.

Focus Without Intensity

The first step is to turn our backs on the distractions that creep into our days.
We practice the art of being focused, not in the sense of concentrating intently, but by keeping our minds on the most important thing.

Certainly, you know people who come into meetings highly agitated.
They speak first and fast. It's as if they need to dump the content of their
thinking on the table immediately and with an emotional charge so that
the rest of us can play with it. All too often, we do. The result is that the
group speeds down the proverbial rabbit trail.

We can attend to the most important thing only by keeping our attention
in the moment. So often we clutter our minds with memories of yesterday's
events or with worries about what might happen tomorrow. Or we rush into
things and become so busy doing "stuff" that we lose perspective. Most self-
defeating of all, we become concerned about how we look to others. All of
this comes with being human and thinking too much about ourselves.

When we move through our days immersed in distractions, it's like we're
trying to find our way through the wilderness with our heads bowed, wearing
blinders to which we've become so accustomed that we've forgotten we're
wearing them. We have a rigidly limited view of possible paths, but keep
pushing our way forward. No matter how many vines we have to cut through
or how many rocks we must climb over, we're going to make it! And because
we're tough and smart and determined, make it we do. But at what cost?
Often, we've so exhausted ourselves and everyone who is trying to follow us
that there is little joy even in reaching our goal. The process has involved too
much drudgery to leave energy for celebration.

Kids Prove the Darnedest Things

The Squirrel Island Tea Shoppe is a small operation that proves a big
point. Open just 52 days a year, it offers lunches and snacks to vaca-
tioners who spend all or part of their summers on this small Maine
island. It's the place to go after the mail arrives to connect with other
Islanders; it's where children come every afternoon for ice cream
after a swim at the beach. And for a group of teenagers, it is their first
summer job.

For three years, the place had been going downhill. Losses
were mounting ($17,000 on revenues of $45,000); customers were

complaining about slow service. The teens saw the place as pure drudgery, and absenteeism rose. One of the supervising adults, in all innocence, made things worse. Trying to push the kids, she'd tell them that they didn't know how to do their jobs and that they needed to "commit to working harder," that they needed to "get a new attitude." The teens persevered, but concluded that work was just something you need to do to earn money so that you can have fun in your free time.

But Sarah, a college student and the Tea Shoppe manager, took her feelings of discouragement as a warning sign; she sought help from two mentors. Their initial advice: focus on the most important, obvious thing that needed to change. Sarah started that immediately. She began to show appreciation for her staff. Small gestures—such as providing customized, silk-screened shirts—lightened the mood.

The kids started coming forward with suggestions. "Let's make use of our electronic cash register," said Ben, a high school student who liked computers. "I'll bet there's stuff it can do to make our jobs easier." Sure enough, Ben programmed the machine to change how orders were processed, shortening the wait for food. Soon the supervising adults began to catch the positive spirit. Instead of criticizing, they began to pitch in—easing whatever bottlenecks developed.

Inevitably, customers picked up on the changes and came more often. After just a few weeks, daily revenues bounced into the black. What had been a slow-motion train wreck had stopped, hung in the balance for a short time, and then reversed direction. The young manager had learned to stay mentally present, grasping that her job was to create the right atmosphere, and then focused on things one step at a time.

What Distracting Thoughts Get in *Your* Way?

The list of distracting habits of thinking could go on and on; each of us engages in our own favorites in an innocent effort to cope with an overload of stimulation and challenges. The strategy of distraction is ultimately futile. Just ask recovering alcoholics. They may have drunk themselves unconscious, tried to numb themselves against difficult thoughts and feelings for years. But the farther they strayed from *presence,* the more problems they encountered— and the less able they were to deal with those problems.

Even when it takes a more benign form than drugs or alcohol, distraction ultimately makes us less effective. From reading trashy novels or TV channel surfing, to shopping or snacking, to computer games or nonstop checking of e-mail and voice mail—we may choose from an infinite number of distractions. The good news is that the antidote is always at our fingertips, what we call *reflective patience.*

High-Wire Prioritizing

Conventional: Hold the Reins	Step Up: Reflective Patience
Marshal intellectual arguments	Entertain fundamental questions about vision, purpose, goals, and strategies
"Ready, fire, aim"	Understand critical issues before acting
Intensity (applied force)	Clarity (dismissal of distractions)
Focused on expectations	Alert as events unfold
Frenzied spinning from crisis to crisis	Seeing the obvious and doing it

---

Eight Habits of Distracted Thinking

- *Worry:* In its misguided way, this is an attempt to control the unknown. We ponder all the things that might happen, as if we can stop the tide just by our thinking.

- *Anger/resentment:* When people in our organization reject or challenge our ideas or suggestions, sometimes we just react. Anger and resentment encourage us to focus on how right we think we are. Such closed-minded resistance actually hampers our ability to work effectively within the flow of events. We become like a fallen water-skier, dragged along by external forces, flailing about and swallowing water.

- *Second-guessing:* Could I have done that better? We revisit the past, dissecting each decision. Such thoughts drain productive energy, as if we're trying to row a boat with only one oar—going 'round and 'round in circles.

- *Guilt:* By saying, "I've screwed up and there's no redemption," guilt causes us to give up hope. We're so busy beating on ourselves that we miss the signal to sail our boat to the starting line of the race.

- *Jumping to conclusions:* We're so intent on inserting ourselves into the conversation that we stop listening to others. Because people can be shy, interruptions may lead them to become too quiet. We miss the chance to get important information and may lose the race by heading in the wrong direction.

- *Assuming intent:* We judge the actions of others without asking what thoughts set them in motion. What is to be gained by yelling at a crew-member who is doing the best she can?

- *Desiring approval:* We constantly perform to an unseen audience, so wrapped up in wondering how we look to the people on shore that we don't see that the current is running against us.

- *Comparison:* Instead of experiencing the moment, we judge it against what's gone before, against our expectations of what could be, against what we imagine to be true for someone else. As if we're sailing into a glorious sunset and wondering if the view would be better from someone else's boat.

Clarity Via Reflective Patience

Those with reflective patience stay easy and alert as things unfold. To achieve this state, we drop our expectations of what should be. We stop comparing to what has happened before, or to what someone else has done or is doing.

Reflective patience is not about suffering in silence or holding steady until things get better. Instead, it empowers us to notice and accept whatever is happening—good, bad, indifferent—with curiosity. Most important, reflective patience means not acting on the urge to kick into effort or control. The more effort and control we try to exert, the more we limit the number of possibilities available to us; it's like quicksand that sucks us in deeper the more we struggle. If we are frantic, other people react with agitation. They cannot connect to us. Even worse, in this mood we cannot connect to our innate creativity, inventiveness, originality. We cut ourselves off from the possibility of a latent solution emerging.

Crisis Mentality

Early in 2004 a health-care provider was really struggling with adversity. Its stock price had dropped by more than 40% in a matter of weeks; the CFO had resigned, and Wall Street expected lower earnings for at least a couple of years.

As they addressed this crisis, the company's leaders set immediate business issues aside—in essence, they were compelled to use their mental back burners. At the next executive meeting, about one month into the events, they were shocked to find a certain calmness. Past personal differences seemed unimportant; past mistakes were forgiven. The crisis, as can be the case, cleared out the mental clutter and gave members of the executive team a composed sense of focus. In one session they agreed on appointing someone to head an effort to satisfy a key customer group, another to streamline support infrastructure, and a third to give renewed emphasis to a stalled initiative to improve procurement. The very next day, one could sense the energy that these simple actions evoked in the ranks.

But don't wait for a crisis to clear your thinking process; far better to use the power of insight when things are going well.

High-Wire Key to Framing the Big Picture: Dismiss Distracting Thoughts

Why choose to dwell in the same old habits, be prisoner of the same old reactions, be caught in the same self-centered cage, or trapped by assumptions? You can learn to respond appropriately to varied situations by using thought as a tool, with the same accomplished skill that a master craftsperson uses a lathe to shape rough wood into something functional and beautiful.

When we turn our back on mental distractions, clarity and focus happen naturally. Seeing this for yourself is all it takes to handle increasing levels of responsibility with ease, keeping your head, to paraphrase Rudyard Kipling, when all about you are losing theirs—and blaming it on you.

Reflective patience is a state of profound but graceful concentration. Completely aware of our own thought processes and simultaneously connected with others, we are able to perform with ingenuity, verve, and spontaneity. With such presence, we may fulfill a manager's fundamental responsibility: unwavering resolve to sustain an environment in which people feel confident enough to do good work.

> We are as our heart's desire is.
> As our heart's desire is, so is our will.
> As our will is, so is our deed.
> As our deed is, so is our destiny.
>
> —The Upanishads,
> the mystic teachings of Hinduism

CHAPTER 12

The Antidote to Stress

Key question: Must I invest heroic amounts of energy to motivate others and gain recognition? Must I sacrifice home, family, friends to succeed?

"I had to worry," Vittoria said recently. She's a senior executive in a company that had just completed its second round of layoffs, struggling to ride out tough economic times. She couldn't shirk her responsibilities, couldn't just shrug her shoulders and wait for some sort of miracle. Important decisions had to be made, and she was one of the people who must make them. The company's problems were real, and team members were counting on her to play a key role in finding solutions. And so, she believed, she had to worry.

How much we worry seems to show how seriously we take an issue, how much we care about it, how much energy we're willing to invest to find a solution. So worry and its attendant stress seem inescapable.

The greatest rewards often seem to go to the most stressed-out workers, as bosses "want to see 'em sweat." Indeed, some people say that stress can be a good thing, a helpful spur to results. Nonsense. The simple truth is that people must feel secure to do their best work. In other words, it's easier to walk—even perform stunts—on the high wire if you know that there's a safety net. By acting as the safety net for their teams, managers inspire better performance.

Begin by cutting thought habits such as worry down to size. For instance, peek behind the curtain, and see how flimsy worry actually is. Like all managers, we're facing an issue or problem. Because we don't know precisely what to do or even exactly what will happen, we're operating in the unknown.

Nipping Stress at the Source

"Shouldn't we sort out the sources of stress?" a colleague asks. "External versus internal, the ones we can't control versus those we can?"

To be blunt: *all stress is internal.*

Yes, we are constantly being bombarded. By interruptions. By people who are rude, who have hidden agendas or different priorities, or who fail to hold up their end. By assignments with short deadlines, changing parameters, inadequate resources, unrealistic goals. The list goes on and on—things outside our control that sap our energy from the job at hand.

But are such things necessarily stressful? Do they inevitably make us suffer? What are the actual dynamics of stress?

Something unplanned happens. It triggers an instinctive response: a rush of adrenaline, faster heartbeat, sweaty palms, butterflies in the stomach. All of that is outside our conscious control. But we have choices about what happens next. Do we get frustrated or stay focused? Take things personally or stay objective? Fret or accept?

Consider the sensations listed above. We are as likely to experience them on an amusement park roller coaster as we are when the bottom drops out of a complex project. Yet we have fun at the amusement park while we feel stressed at the office.[1]

You will never be able to control all the external factors, or even all your physiological and emotional responses to the unexpected. But there is no stress—no suffering—until we engage negative *thinking.*

That's why conventional efforts to "manage stress" fall short; we get better at sorting issues into neat piles, but continue to be whipsawed. There's no real relief—unless and until we change our *internal* game. When we reset our mental default to *Reflective Mode* (as described in figure 6.1 on page 66), we become more resilient.

And that nips stress at the source.

That means that we're a little unsure. And because our minds are naturally fertile, we start thinking about all the bad things that could happen, all the consequences that could play out. In our imaginations, the seed of concern grows larger and larger. That's worry: imagination fertilizing insecurity until we raise a tangled thicket of thorny thoughts.

But the executive we met at the start of this chapter has found a way to stop her negative thought habit—worry—from generating stress. What's helping? "Just knowing that worry is a thought," she says.

As simple as that sounds, it isn't always easy. We are so used to the chatter in our heads that we forget a simple truth: as events are happening, anticipated consequences aren't yet real.

Freedom of thought—the faculty to choose what we dwell on—was ably demonstrated by Edwin Moses, the great hurdler. Sometimes he felt so concerned before a race that he became physically ill. But when anxiety crept up on him, he found that he could ease its affect by simply not paying attention to it. As he let go of the focus on worry, Moses' mind relaxed. In that more peaceful state, he found the confidence—even joy—to perform well; the only barriers left to overcome were the actual physical hurdles. Moses won five Olympic medals and was undefeated in his specialty for ten years—arguably one of the greatest achievements in sports history.[2]

Courage: Going Ahead Anyway

Martin, the CFO of a global consumer packaged goods company, walked down the steps from the stage and into the audience. "Sure, I have been scared over this past year, uncertain that we were doing the right thing in globalizing our infrastructure. I have lain awake at night wondering how we were going to get everything done. And I have been worried about my future—knowing I would be fired if we could not close the books, if our line managers did not have the information they need to run the business."

The room went completely silent. You could hear a pin drop. Not one of the 150 people moved. For Martin was actually saying what everyone at the meeting had felt at one time or another during the past 12 months. That he actually *acknowledged it himself* had them spellbound. He was their leader, after all. Not supposed to have doubt. Not expected to worry. He exuded such confidence, had such charisma, was so smart. Surely he had nothing to fear. He could never be stressed; he couldn't get depressed.

Martin turned around and climbed up the staircase to the stage and then said, "But you know something? When I catch myself feeling distressed, I only need remind myself that we are headed in the right direction; even more important, that I am completely confident in your abilities to get us where we need to go. That gives me the vigor to keep forging ahead."

Even Anger

In any discussion of stress, anger merits special attention. Many people believe that "letting off steam" can help alleviate stress, or that it can activate a kind of good stress, thereby becoming a motivational tool. "Anger gives me the energy to fight back," says one of our clients. "America had to get angry after 9/11 so that we could do the job that had to be done in Afghanistan."

Really? Are bombs more effective if the flight crews who drop them are not just determined, but angry? Beyond that, is anger really helpful?

Angry thoughts can cause an adrenaline rush that gives the illusion of creative energy. Angry thoughts are compelling. But they consume our attention, blinding us to many possible choices. When we're in that state—literally, a "blind rage"—it's harder for us to tap our most helpful resources: intuition, common sense, wisdom. It can be particularly hard to keep our bearings when faced with anger and disapproval—or even distraction—by people in authority. The power of position seems to give special weight to the boss's words.

But no matter how high the position from which they come, words are simply expressions of thoughts. Sure, it's common for a boss to be absolutely insistent about doing things a certain way, or about setting out to achieve a particular goal. That reflects the fact that the leader's willpower is an essential ingredient for the success of her organization.

A difficult boss doesn't see her thought processes; they've become habits. All of us find it easy to acknowledge that we are creatures of habit in what we *do*—following the same routine every morning, taking the same route to work every day, and so on. But do we also see that we are enthralled by our own *thinking* habits?

Meanwhile, employees pay careful attention to what the leader says and does. So the boss's habitual thoughts cause all kinds of compensating behaviors.

You don't have to work that way. Resist knee-jerk reactions to the boss. Remember that she is simply a person who, like all of us, can get gripped by unpleasant thoughts.

When You Can't Just Hang Up

A newly promoted director of communications of a global packaged goods company joined a conference call between the firm's CFO and two vendors trying to win a small contract. The call did not go well. Ultimately, the CFO interrupted: "Look," he said brusquely, "you must understand one thing if you are going to work with me—when I ask a question, I expect you to answer the question I asked, not the one you wanted to answer."

Ouch. Time to crawl under the chair, or maybe just hang up. Fortunately, one of the vendors was able to keep his mental bearings while the other knew enough to be still. By not reacting to the CFO's pique, the two were able to rewind the conversation to the moment before the blowup and play through the question with a fresh start.

As soon as the call ended, the director of communications rang up the vendors. "My boss just doesn't understand how intimidating he can be," she said. "If you guys think that call was hard, imagine what it is like for those of us who have to go into his office every day. What did you do to get him calmed down so quickly—I thought he was going to blow!"

One of the vendors responded, "Well, we just stayed calm by remembering that anyone can lose his mental well-being from time to time."

And when *you* are acting as boss, your challenge is exactly the same—to decouple yourself from your positional authority and relate to others just as one human does to another. Truly, we are all equal in striving to do the best we can in the face of our own foibles and insecurities.

Anti-Stress Choice #1: Defuse Anger with Forgiveness

Even in situations where we seem to have little control, we can make choices that defuse stress.

Consider Nelson Mandela, a man who had a lot of reason to be angry. For more than half a century, Mandela led the movement against apartheid, the government policy by which South Africa's white minority persecuted the black majority. By 1961, when he was sent to prison, Mandela had concluded that armed struggle was inevitable as a defense against the violence of apartheid. For more than 20 years, he held to that view, even rejecting an offer of release from prison if he would renounce violence.

Mandela played a significant role in the ultimate demise of apartheid. Pundits credit not his anger but his eventual turn to patience, wisdom, vision, and integrity. When he was finally released from prison in February 1990, Mandela said: "I call in the strongest possible way for us to act with the dignity and discipline that our just struggle for freedom deserves." And on Christmas Eve of that year, Mandela addressed his nation: "We must strive to be moved by a generosity of spirit that will enable us to outgrow the hatred and conflict of the past."[3]

Another word for that "generosity of spirit" is not usual in the business context. It is, simply, forgiveness. Forgiveness doesn't mean that we condone

---

Calculating the return on anger

- What positive outcomes have you accomplished when you were angry?
- What "collateral damage" occurred?
- Are you satisfied with the return on the time and energy you have invested in angry thoughts?

bad decisions or harmful behaviors. It doesn't mean that we will forget, or that we won't hold accountable the perpetrators of misdeeds. It doesn't mean that we won't act vigorously to take care of ourselves and others and to make things right. But we can do what needs to be done far more effectively—and with far less stress—if we are thinking clearly than if we are angry and resentful.

"When boys throw mean words at you, it is as if they are throwing a ball at the wall; they expect you to react by bouncing back," a sixth-grade teacher advised Bob's son Remy when he was being teased about a mistake. "But you can decide not to do that. You can choose what you think, instead of feeling that you always have to bounce back at them in anger."

Anti-Stress Choice #2: Deflect Blame with Humility

Mastering the ability to keep our bearings when everything hits the fan can begin with giving up the need to defend our image. Let's face it: we all make mistakes. Trying to keep that a secret (as if we could!) takes enormous amounts of energy. We liberate that energy through humility.

Consider, for example, the pressure that surrounds annual budget planning. At a typical communications company, it was a three-month process that climaxed with a presentation by the director and financial manager of the business unit at headquarters. In a half-day grilling, the CEO, COO, CFO, and CAO would rehash the current year's successes and failures and then dissect the proposed budget line-by-line, down to questioning the rationale for raises to individual secretaries.

One year, the overall performance of Jo's business unit had been strong. But she had made a bad hire—a team leader who had alienated subordinates, failed to win the confidence of key customers, and offended peers. Within five months, Jo had terminated him, costing the firm thousands of dollars in severance fees and charge-offs. Jo wasn't surprised when the annual planning conversation turned to the bad hire. The COO waxed eloquent about the mistake, his voice rising higher and higher as his words came faster and faster. Jabbing his finger in Jo's face, he demanded, "How could you let this happen?"

Talk about stress! Jo's career flashed before her eyes. What could she do?

In the grip of anxiety, she could have become defensive, something like this:

> Well, it really wasn't so bad. It only cost us a few thousand dollars, and we still beat plan this year. . . . And his credentials looked good. . . . And everybody kept saying we had to find a team leader quick, fast, and in a hurry, or we'd start losing

business. . . . And, I wasn't the only one who interviewed him. . . . And, besides, what about all the *other* people who had to be terminated in other offices?

Any of those volleys would lead to a forceful return—defensiveness offending the people on whose good opinion Jo depended.

But instead of *reacting,* Jo took a mental breath. In a split second, she *saw* that the COO's thoughts were spinning, and she *chose* not to follow suit. So she answered the COO's challenging question—"How could you let that happen?"—with her honest feeling. In a steady voice, she dryly remarked: "Well, it seemed like a good idea at the time."

The COO, who had been drawing breath for his next point, stopped short and blinked. The others laughed; the COO laughed; Jo laughed. In that single instant, the feeling in the room changed. Jo's choice switched the meeting from blame-and-defense over one mistake to collaboration on the bigger picture.

High-Wire Stress Management

Conventional: Exhausted

Your mind runs in a loop. Addressing a problem, you find yourself going over and over the same data.

Your thoughts come faster and faster, until you don't even have time to catch a breath.

You are *absolutely certain* that you *must* look at the issue *this way.*

Your underlying feeling is insecurity.

Step Up: Energized

You sift information only so long as you are discovering new connections.

Your thinking is steady and clear. It feels like you have plenty of time.

You are curious about more options.

Your underlying feeling is confidence—for no good reason.

Anti-Stress Choice #3: Take It Home

The understanding we are talking about doesn't just reduce stress at work. It also makes a difference in what we take home with us. In other words, it's important in work/life balance.

Has a loved one ever asked you, "How was your day, dear?" only to elicit your response: "I don't want to talk about it"? Yet your internal dialogue goes on. Your body is at home, eating dinner, watching TV. But where is your mind? Going over and over the events of the day just past or the demands of the next? In other words, is your thinking driving a wedge between you and the people close to you?

That happened often at Betsy's house. It was hard for her to "leave it at the office." The tension was most obvious when her husband, Gary, was trying to be the nicest. Early in her career, Betsy would travel about once every other month. On her return, she'd look forward to being met at the gate by her husband. Mind you, it's an hour drive from their house to the airport—over the Golden Gate Bridge, through the city of San Francisco, down the freeway to the airport. Gary had a flexible work schedule, and he didn't mind.

After a while, they noticed a strange pattern. Betsy's plane would land; she and Gary would hug and kiss and head for home. But more often than not, by the time they got to the Golden Gate Bridge, they'd be squabbling. They'd missed each other, looked forward to getting back together. What was going on?

They got the answer from a lecture that Gary attended. He heard that anthropologists have studied tribes in Africa where the men would go out weeks at a time hunting for food. When they returned, they did not swagger directly into their village, full of aggressive excitement. Instead, the lecturer said, the hunters pitched a camp just outside the village. They stayed there for a day or two, watching the women, children, and old people come and go. Only when they felt in synch with the mild rhythm of daily life did they return to their homes.

Business travelers—"road warriors"—are not unlike those African hunters. For days at a time, we're cut loose from homey tasks—making the bed, grocery shopping, walking the dog, taking out the garbage. We focus our energies on meetings, phone calls, presentations. It's challenging and stimulating; it engages all of our wit and energy.

Meanwhile, our loved ones are just as engaged in the tasks in front of them—everything it takes to keep a home and family going, as well as their own work. Their days, too, require all their wit and energy.

Two partners, each involved in activities that contribute to their joint well-being. But we're operating at different speeds, in different environments, on different wavelengths. Is it any surprise that we clash when we get back together?

Here's another metaphor for this phenomenon: a canal. Picture two bodies of water separated by a narrow strip of land. To transfer boats smoothly between them, you need a canal—a series of locks that gradually lift or lower a boat coming from Ocean A until it's at the same level as Sea B. People, like boats, need level waters.

So how far do you have to go, how long do you have to be away, to experience the stress of "unlevel waters?" Not long and not far. One trip to the office, or even a conference call at home, can take us away, because the important "trip" happens in our minds.

So Betsy now wheels her own suitcase through the airport and secures transportation to her front door. She gives Gary a quick kiss, pats the dog, changes her clothes, checks out the mail, and pads around the house for an hour or so. Gary is there, within reach, quietly doing his thing. When the "waters" feel level, the two engage. Betsy is still putting miles on the relationship. But now there are fewer bumps in the road.

Insulating from Work Stress

At the office...
- Notice your mental tone from time to time.
- Build in a few moments during the day to create just a little breathing room between you and your thoughts.
- Leave your desk and walk around the block, or just around the building.
- If you have a couple of minutes between meetings or phone calls, don't check your e-mail; just sit and breathe deeply.

As you transition home...
- Pay attention to the people and buildings you pass; cultivate a feeling of fascination.
- If on public transportation, read the comic pages of the newspaper or something else that makes you laugh.
- If driving, turn off the ignition and sit in your car for just a moment before you walk in the door. Bring your attention to the present, with gratitude for the ones you love.[4]

High-Wire Key to Reducing Stress: Change Thinking, Change Feeling, Change Behavior—Change Outcomes

Workplace stress costs in excess of $300 billion annually, estimates the American Institute of Stress, in health care, time off, and lost productivity.[5] No wonder there's so much talk about stress management!

But resiliency is a far better strategy. We see this in the world of physical fitness. In the 1980s and '90s, we were urged to "feel the burn." Now, "no pain, no gain" workouts are giving way to yoga and its admonition to "meet yourself with compassion." If you experience physical pain, a yogi explains, your muscles tighten in a kind of instinctual defense. The more you try to work through pain, the stiffer your body gets.

Same with stress. The more you fret, the more rigid your thinking gets. We are not suggesting that any of us can wish away concerns about all the tasks for which we are responsible. We are not, in short, proposing "positive thinking" or "affirmations." Our thoughts flow continuously, like a river, and we can no more shut them off than we can stop the Nile. Try to sit completely still for even one minute. Notice how much of the time you are distracted by a thought, any kind of thought: happy, sad, judgment, observation, memory, fact. That mental chatter goes on and on.

We consider, contemplate, compare, contrast, cogitate, conclude, categorize, conceptualize, analyze, summarize, theorize, intellectualize, rationalize, reason, ruminate, speculate, suppose, study. We ponder and puzzle, muse and mull over. We deliberate, debate, and deduce. We have random thoughts, idle thoughts, trains of thought, after thoughts, and second thoughts. We think even when we sleep.

Negative thoughts inevitably crowd in sometimes, one after the other, tumbling over each other. If someone said, "Your job is to haul out each one of your negative thoughts and re-paint it positive," you'd know you were doomed to fail—if only by exhaustion. Sooner or later, you'd be unable to sustain the effort with the small part of your brain that you consciously control. A colleague recently said, for example, "I try to dwell on my happy memories," then paused and added, "because there were so many bad ones." Clearly, her technique—"think happy thoughts"—left open a trapdoor!

But, remember, we can choose what we dwell on. When we stay attuned to the fact that *they are just my thoughts,* we don't have to fall victim to stress.

> Men are disturbed not by things that happen, but by their opinions of the things that happen.
>
> Epictetus, Greek Stoic, 55–135

CHAPTER 13

Measuring Up

Key question: Now that the stakes are higher, how should I
be evaluated?

Instead of resting on his laurels, a 40-year GE veteran challenged his own
performance. He was already effective, running a 2,500-person organization
that delivered essential services to various GE divisions at a 50% savings. His
shop was innovative, highly acknowledged outside the company. But might
he have some "flat spots?" He decided to ask his organization, in a series of
town hall meetings, for feedback about his own performance. What he heard
astounded him.

Staff pointed out that he micromanaged many tasks and spent far too
much time on inconsequential issues. Imagine hearing that unadulterated
assessment—and in public forums, no less!

A few months later Bob happened to catch him in his office. "I can't
believe how well my division is performing," he said. "Ever since I got serious
about setting clearer priorities for myself and worrying less about whether my
people were doing their jobs, our numbers have gone through the roof."

In other words, the feedback he received caused him to rethink his leadership style. As he gave up micromanagement of such areas as the operating
centers, for example, he found more time and energy for longer-reaching
issues, such as expanding the service offering, embedding Six Sigma[1]
methodologies, and making fundamental improvements in the customer's
experience by using more self-service tools. His personal leadership on these
issues communicated to the entire organization that these were important

priorities. Not only did opportunities open up, but this manager also got an excellent handle on the competence of his people to bring changes to life. Where they struggled, he helped out; when they ran into roadblocks, he had the time to intervene; when they lacked resources, he found them.

"By giving my staff permission to give me direct feedback, I find it so easy to do my job," this manager observed. "Literally, I rely on them to give me the information I need to self-correct. It's wonderful to be able to work so openly and frankly, feeling so connected. My stress level has gone way down."

High-Wire Metrics

Conventional: Numbers Game	Step Up: Making Intangibles Tangible
Short-term financial results	Quality of decision-making
	Speed of *appropriate* action
	Pace of innovation
	Level of employees' commitment and initiative
	Level of customer loyalty

The GE executive cited above is a good example of the dictum that managers need to spend about 90% of their time leading and only 10% actually "working" (i.e., accomplishing tasks). Once we step up to a certain level, our performance should be measured not so much by what we personally do, build, or create, but by whether we set the right tone and the proper conditions so that *others* step forward with conviction in the face of change, demands for results, and unexpected events.

Of course, the more invested a manager becomes in his group's success, the harder it is to point to his individual accomplishments—to say that *this* specific effort yielded *that* portion of the ultimate return. So how should managers be evaluated?

#1: How Well Do You Unleash Collective Energy?

Tony, the executive vice president of HR for one of the mega retailers (more than 900 stores) was sitting in a leadership team meeting when the CEO smacked the table and expounded, "I just don't get why we have a handful of stores that consistently outperform the others. What are they doing? Frustrates the hell out of me—if we could only bottle the magic we would be well on our way to beating our 5% margin goal!"

Taking the CEO's challenge to find the link to store performance seriously, Tony created an elegant framework. He started with a simple, but easily taken for granted, premise—customers were more likely to continue to shop where they had enjoyed themselves and gotten what they wanted. So Tony gathered data that allowed him to correlate store profitability with *customer loyalty*. His results proved that every five points of measured customer satisfaction resulted in a 1% increase in store profitability.

But he did not stop there. Then Tony asked, "What factors caused high customer satisfaction?" Not surprisingly, the data showed a correlation with high levels of employee satisfaction. In other words, happy employees are nicer to customers. Again, this proved the intuitively obvious. But just by quantifying what the leaders of this institution had long suspected, the research had a big impact.

"What factors resulted in high employee satisfaction?" That was the next question to be researched. The correlation was with *store manager effectiveness*.

Finally! Tony had an answer that hung together. He expressed it in this formula:

$$\text{Profits} = \text{customer satisfaction} \times \text{employee satisfaction}$$
$$\times \text{ manager effectiveness}$$

Manager effectiveness was determined by straightforward questions (see list below for the type of questions used). Nothing complicated, just the basic questions about behaviors that good store managers exhibit—as defined by the employees. Notice that they point to *respect*—acknowledgment of the principle that each of us is doing the best we can based on our current thinking. Implicit is the understanding that good managers must accommodate the "separate realities" created by the personal thinking of each individual on the team.

The CEO and his team spent the next three years acting on this information, and the company's performance steadily improved. Return on sales increased from 2.1% to 5.8%. Oh—and the stock price nearly doubled.

12 Employee-Defined Measures of Store Manager Effectiveness

- Does your manager ask your opinion on how a task should be accomplished?
- Does your manager treat the employees with respect?
- Do you enjoy your work?
- Does your manager help you when you need it?

- Does your manager understand your job?
- Are issues/problems dealt with promptly and fairly?
- Does your manager say what he/she means, and do what he/she says?
- Is your manager clear about what needs to be accomplished?
- Does your manager enjoy his/her job?
- Does your manager resolve conflicts well?
- Do you feel part of the manager's team?
- Do you believe your manager has your best interests at heart?

#2: How Well Do You Focus Attention and Mental Energy?

As Warren Buffet has noted, there is no more powerful force in nature than the power of compounding returns. For example, a 10% return will multiply the proverbial $10,000 investment sixfold over a 15-year time horizon ($62,600). Similarly, small performance improvements by employees will multiply over time to yield spectacularly better outcomes.

But how can managers predict which small points will provide big leverage? In other words, how do you know where to focus?

Focus, itself, became the crux of measurement by a mega bank in the United States. One of its core management processes is based on the Hoshin planning system—a methodology used by such Japanese companies as Toyota as part of their ongoing quality efforts. Goals, objectives, and actions cascade right from the top. First, the CEO articulates his main goals and describes the broad actions to achieve them. Then, the managers of each business unit and function use the framework to set their own objectives and actions so that the link between the focus of every department and that of the company is crystal clear.

Adding teeth to the process, each action has a metric—sometimes quantitative, other times qualitative—so progress can be tracked. Quarterly, managers take the Hoshin framework and relate the actions taken and progress made for each principal objective. They describe their own initiatives and deeds during the period, categorizing them into four buckets—essential, beneficial, neutral, and negligible. Once each manager has produced a draft based on his own perceptions, he shares this with his staff. Some people feel more comfortable doing this face-to-face, others ask for feedback via e-mail, still others facilitate communication with greater anonymity.

Whatever procedure is used, the manager usually ends up with a table that looks something like table 13.1, taken from an actual assessment. It

TABLE 13.1

Linking Department and Company Focus

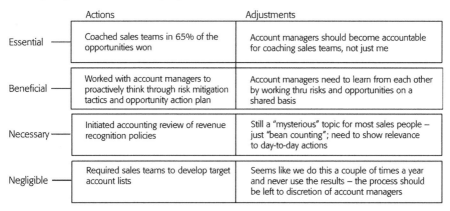

	Actions	Adjustments
Essential	Coached sales teams in 65% of the opportunities won	Account managers should become accountable for coaching sales teams, not just me
Beneficial	Worked with account managers to proactively think through risk mitigation tactics and opportunity action plan	Account managers need to learn from each other by working thru risks and opportunities on a shared basis
Necessary	Initiated accounting review of revenue recognition policies	Still a "mysterious" topic for most sales people – just "bean counting"; need to show relevance to day-to-day actions
Negligible	Required sales teams to develop target account lists	Seems like we do this a couple of times a year and never use the results – the process should be left to discretion of account managers

clearly depicts the manager's performance based on her actions during the quarter, and it expresses the adjustments she can make that may have a positive result in the next period.

As should be obvious from merely reading the results of the manager depicted here, the true power comes from the process used to identify and categorize fruitful actions and then to explore the adjustments going forward. Essentially, the process allows the manager to see where she is having impact—and where she needs to concentrate her efforts in the near future.

For this company, the effect of focus has been galvanizing. The feedback is thoughtful, direct, and immediate. One lesson is that by keeping the attention on results and allowing employees to assess actions using an effectiveness scale, managers have specific information necessary to see where their actions correlate with constructive outcomes and where they are having virtually no impact. Managers are learning what actions actually make a difference, as seen by people throughout the organization.

#3: How Well Do You Make Adjustments Based on Feedback?

Have you ever had an employee come to you and say, "You know boss, I really achieved only 73% of my productive capacity today, but I'll do better tomorrow"? Ever tried to assess your own performance—even just the amount of effort you put in, much less actual work output? Difficult, isn't it? Not too many of us have jobs where the link between effort and result is unequivocal.

What To Measure on the High Wire—
Management Competence Applied to:

- Motivating effectively
- Leading by example
- Creating a positive tone
- Coaching/giving feedback
- Communicating
- Paying attention/focus
- Being respectful
- Acting with character
- Getting expected results

Every good manager needs continuous feedback; it can help enhance performance. But it won't mean a thing if we aren't in the right frame of mind: open, curious. And that means, as we've seen, being able to take ourselves lightly, to be comfortable listening quietly to others without feeling defensive or justifying our behaviors, to be secure enough to let go of our need to know everything.

But anyone who has occupied a manager's chair knows how little helpful feedback one gets during the course of a day. In fact, being promoted often means the end of virtually *all* feedback. The manager's boss assumes that the results will speak for themselves—either you will or you won't deliver. The staff is not accustomed to giving their assessments, either because they are afraid of retribution or the possibility is not even in their consciousness.

So, many companies institutionalize 360-degree feedback instruments in which employees can assess the boss. But these can fall prey to overkill— "What exactly am I supposed to do with feedback about 85 behavioral traits?" And they may mistakenly put the emphasis on the *content* of assessment, which is less important than the manager's commitment to routinely and directly solicit feedback from an *open stance*—looking through someone else's mental frame and then considering appropriate action in response.

We are all human, fallible; we are vulnerable to our own thinking. By giving others the power to comment on our behavior and effectiveness, we go a long way toward self-correction; we have the chance to change before patterns become ingrained. Feedback informs intervention before our thoughts become habits that limit our choices and shrink our possibilities.

Believe It or Not: There's Profit in the Intangibles

All this might seem a bit simplistic—improve the mood and business results inevitably follow. But once the leadership at the eponymous firm that Bob founded focused on the kinds of *intangibles* we've been discussing, a *tangible* shift occurred in performance.

Quarterly meetings showed the difference. The staff was more engaged; people laughed more, yet were able to complete the formal agenda in a fraction of the time. What had been all-day meetings became three- to four-hour working sessions. Somehow, all the critical issues got discussed, decisions got made, and actions formulated. Even more important, mindsets shifted—aligning the collective thinking to the firm's needs and objectives.

As the staff enjoyed their jobs more, clients began commenting on how easy we were to work with. They let us know just how unique our team was, compared to the traditional consultants who always seem to skulk around in a somber mood. And that facilitated the changes our customers wanted to make. One client team, for example, started out highly dysfunctional: colleagues were barely speaking with each other. Its work pattern was transformed to the extent that, in an executive review session, the team actually made a presentation in skit format and had the senior executives laughing along with them.

And while all this "touchy-feely stuff" was happening, our firm's financial performance got better and better. The business model had suggested that bonuses could equal 100% of base compensation, but actual results had been stuck in the 30% to 40% range. As the thinking of the firm's managers improved, performance took off—ultimately, the bonus was as much as 120% of base.

High-Wire Key to Evaluation: Hard Results from "Soft Stuff"

Every newly appointed or promoted manager wants to accomplish something noteworthy. Is that possible in light of the everyday pressures that seem to leave no choice but to pull out all the stops to deliver good numbers? Even the cubicle walls seem to whisper: "survival of the fittest...dog eat dog...nice guys finish last." And yet, some highly successful companies talk about deep feelings and the precepts we've addressed throughout this book. Johnson & Johnson's Credo starts with the words, "Our first responsibility is to the doctors, nurses and patients, to mothers and fathers and all others who use our products." That hasn't stopped J&J from increasing earnings at more than 11% per year for more than 100 years!

Such results are sustainable only when leaders and managers are held accountable for liberating people's passion to engage fully in the enterprise's mission—to unreservedly give it their best effort.

Men have looked away from themselves and at things so long . . . [that] they measure their esteem of each other by what each has, and not what each is.

—Ralph Waldo Emerson

CHAPTER 14

Wellspring

Key question: How can I sustain energy in the face of limitless demands on my time?

Joanne became one of those people who develop a "1,000-yard stare." Six
months after she took on new management responsibilities, the demands of
the job simply overwhelmed her reserves. She was tapped out. Done. Baked.
Toast.

Joanne had been running a call center, having moved up from the phones to
the corner office. Nearly 200 people worked for her, with the issues—scheduling,
absenteeism, and high turnover—that mark such operations. Spending eight
hours a day resolving peoples' problems can be a burnout job. Yet Joanne was
doing fabulously—loved coming to work, solving the mini-crises that cropped
up throughout the day, often turning out the lights when the hot-line hours
were over. The days flew by, and Joanne felt contented. She was the epitome
of the hands-on manager, and her people loved her for it.

That is, until she was made the VP and General Manager for all call
centers in North America. Now she had four sites, in two countries, and nearly
600 people in her command. At first, Joanne tried to be everywhere at once.
People in her own center became resentful as Joanne spent more and more
time traveling or on the phone. Her admin developed a stock phrase when
someone was looking for her: "She's in a meeting, and I am not sure when it
will be over." Must have been repeated 25 times a day.

Joanne's replacement at her "home" operation could not fill her shoes—no
one could, for Joanne had been the heart and soul of that center. Performance

numbers started falling at Joanne's original operation and at every other center. She felt powerless to stop the trend as she ran from task to task, meeting to meeting, urgent page to urgent page. Joanne grieved for the days when work had seemed so fulfilling and enjoyable, and actually wished she had never earned a promotion.

Joanne was succumbing to a mental trap. She assumed that keeping her mental activity high all day long was a good thing. In other words, she celebrated, as so many of us do, her mastery of multitasking. She was proud of it, for it appeared to give her the vigor to fight fires and get the job done. But multitasking kept Joanne on the surface of issues—like an insect skittering across a pond, rarely probing the deeper questions that might have led to better ways of doing the job in the first place. That kind of busyness worked well when Joanne was a big fish in the pond where she grew up. But when she was promoted into the "ocean," Joanne literally was "at sea."

It had simply not occurred to her that there might be a different way.

> Mental capacity emanates from whatever you choose to call the energy of life itself. We tap into this power by paying attention to the quality of our thinking.

The Inexhaustible Power of a Quiet Mind

Joanne's busymindedness was an energy-draining thought habit (like those described in chapter 11). Such thought habits act like a clogged water filter in the mind. Just as water backs up, decision making stagnates. But as soon as the filter is cleared, fresh thoughts begin flowing.

Everyone knows this feeling. Perhaps you find it when showering, driving the car, praying, playing with your children or your pet. Or perhaps when you wake up and walk outside. Warmth flows through your body; you feel relaxed, yet attentive. As these feelings become more pronounced, your entire mental framework shifts. Fresh ideas emerge without effort; they just pop into your head. Problems that seemed overwhelming in a lesser state of mind suddenly seem like "nothing at all."

Where do such feelings and thoughts come from?

There is an infinite wellspring of wisdom, "gut instinct," creativity. Each of us is born with a channel that doesn't show up on X-rays, but that connects us to that wellspring. We can never lose it or even damage it. But from moment to moment, our channel may become more open or constricted.

An open channel to our clearminded state enables managers, leaders, and executives to deploy the intangible levers of power in service of the institution's aims. These are not learned management tools or methods for getting from point A to point B. Rather, they come from an inner resource that is accessible to all of us if we only slow down our busy minds.

In a nutshell, these levers consist of:

Clarity, springing from insight

Declaration, being awake to your purpose

Enrollment, aligning people behind your goals

Execution, sustaining the energy to get the job done.

You can become expert at recognizing these states by noticing feelings. Clarity manifests in confidence and surefootedness. Declaration is unshakable faith and courage. Enrollment is seen in gratitude as people wholeheartedly put their energy into the cause not only because of external incentives but also because they want to feel part of something larger than themselves. Execution manifests in the exhilaration that transcends personal pride.

In other words, the presence of profound feelings signals our state of mind and our ability to access our inexhaustible energy reserves. In lower states of mind—such as confusion, anxiety, despair—the channel narrows. In higher states of mind—calm, exhilaration, inspiration—it opens wide.

High-Wire Energy

Conventional: Busy	Step Up: Sure
Reacting to urgency	Probing beneath the surface to gain perspective on the important
Looking over our shoulders, hoping to repeat past success	*Knowing* that new answers will appear
Relying on acquired, personal capabilities (knowledge, skills)	Relying on earned capabilities *plus* inborn capacity connected to the wellspring

How to Re-Direct a Busy Mind

Mental States Barometer

Regularly ask yourself:

- Am I looking inside and noticing my emotional state?
- What am I feeling right now?
- Do I find comfortable feelings, giving me a sense of well-being?

- Or do I feel uncomfortable, edgy, stressed?
- Am I remembering that I am the thinker, that I have freedom of choice in shaping my own moment-to-moment experience?

As you become aware of your thought patterns and feelings, you can adjust your behavior, resulting in a positive feedback loop. For Joanne, whom we met at the start of this chapter, mastery of her VP role began with recognition of that effect. Her first step was to identify the feeling associated with being *busyminded:* an imaginary hand pressing against her back, right between her shoulder blades, urging her onward, pushing her from task to task. Awareness of such physical and emotional clues helped Joanne sense a busyminded mood coming. Then, she took preventive action—usually by taking a short break and walking around her building.

Being around too many people jazzed her emotions, making it hard to stay present and calm during the day. Joanne asked her admin to keep her schedule more open and to limit the length of most meetings to 30 minutes.

Sleeping seven to eight hours became a priority, for Joanne noticed that when she was tired, she slipped into busyness more easily. The TV went to the study, out of the bedroom. Joanne also began eating regularly instead of skipping meals. Hunger—like fatigue—left her vulnerable to busymindedness.

Joanne began to change. In a matter of a few weeks, periods of busyminded thinking happened less frequently. She started feeling much more productive and began getting more satisfaction in leading her people.

The benefits rippled outward. People started letting Joanne know what a good job she was doing and how much they liked working for her. The mood of the entire organization lifted; calls seemed to go better, people were much warmer and friendlier with each other and the customers. Not surprisingly, then, performance numbers started moving in the right direction.

Even more startling, though, was something Joanne began to notice about six months later: clarity. As she guided her mind toward tranquility, Joanne found it easier and easier to focus her attention, like a spotlight, on whatever needed to be resolved. Extraneous thoughts occasionally flitted across her mind, but since she had learned not to pay much attention to them, they quickly passed.

Joanne realized that she could focus her mind in a certain direction—on an important issue or even a trivial matter, such as lost car keys. Different from straining to force an answer, this was a kind of mental holding—setting an *intention* for an answer and then staying open to what might emerge. More often than not, an insight would pop. In that instant Joanne would know exactly what to do, or where her keys were hiding.

Working with other people also profoundly changed. The more present Joanne became, the more engaged and clearminded her direct reports became. Her "magic" rubbed off on others—a natural consequence as her leadership evoked confidence among her staff. More and more people discovered the ability to focus their thinking and generate the insights necessary to ever-improving results. Others now accomplished many of the tasks that Joanne used to take on. Sometimes it became apparent that they were just busywork—in fact, they did not really need doing after all.

Joanne found herself saying less and less as the staff increasingly solved issues themselves. Not having to deal with everyone's mental chatter, the team could find a creative solution quickly—and put it into action smoothly—when a real opportunity arose or big decision needed to be made.

In short, by making the mental space to quiet her own thinking and tap into the wellspring, Joanne discovered that she multiplied her management energy. She got better results for far less effort.

Inevitability, we slip off the beam from time to time. After all, we are only human. Thoughts come too fast for us to be able to stop or deflect them. As managers, when we notice ourselves reacting negatively—saying harsh words, feeling pressure—that is the clue that we have lost our connection to mental goodwill and the wellspring of energy. With that awareness, we can choose not to dwell on our negative thoughts. Pretty soon our thinking clears, and we regain our mental equilibrium—and our energy. That is the secret Joanne learned over the course of those months as she was changing. For her, managing will never be the same old, uncomfortable task it once was.

The Manager as Hostess

The late Jane Young Wallace, the first woman vice president of Cahners Publishing Co. and editor/publisher of *Restaurants & Institutions* magazine in the 1970s and 1980s, managed her staff like a hostess at a dinner party. It was her responsibility to place people at the table with companions who could bring out their best, to direct the flow of work so that each person had just the right amount on their plate, and then to ask the kinds of questions that would invite lively dialogue, allowing each voice to be heard but no single person to dominate.

Often, an employee would literally sit at a long dining board set up in Jane's office instead of a typical conference table. He would talk through the pros and cons of an issue. Occasionally, Jane would ask a question. In many conversations, she would simply nod and listen. Yet the employee left satisfied, for Jane applied the hostess's knack to management: she created a welcoming environment and made room for each employee's innate wisdom to offer up answers.

High-Wire Key to Sustaining Energy:
Willpower with Humility

Managers who count on the wellspring see that it helps them discharge their work responsibilities with supreme effectiveness but little or no strain. Operating consistently from a high-minded state is a question of having the humility to recognize when our thinking has slipped off center and the willpower to stay committed to self-awareness.

Willpower is necessary because changing longstanding habits takes practice. It's not enough simply to wish one's mental state were more elevated. As Joanne learned, once having tasted the quiet-minded experience and her transcendent intelligence, she had to make changes in her routines to stay grounded. (Of course, when she started to feel wonderful and work became easier, she got an incentive to stick with this path.)

Your ego is like a monkey on the back of the elephant of your mind, leading it here and there, creating havoc along the way. Put the monkey in his place: make him hang on to your tail and follow your intention.

The process takes perseverance. But, in the metaphor of the high wire, we know that even though we can't see it, there is a safety net under us. And that assurance spurs sustainable enthusiasm as we step into the unknown.

It is the belief in a power larger than myself and other than myself which allows me to venture into the unknown, and even the unknowable.

—Maya Angelou

Afterword: Why Lead?

Key question: Is the effort to walk the wire worth it?

Imagine, for a moment, working for a manager who is kind, calm, steadfast, certain, trustworthy, and spontaneous. Someone who believes that people's actions are performed with good intentions, that people try their best in light of how they see things. Who does not become frightened or upset when things are going badly, or when others are anxious. Who can see outcomes clearly even when the path to them is obscured. Who is willing to change direction when it becomes obvious that there is a better way. Who has your best interests at heart, and who would never deliberately cause you harm.

Now dream that your organization achieves tremendous success as measured by revenue and profit growth, customer satisfaction, innovative products, and ever-improving productivity.

Perhaps you have worked at a company that achieved success under the kind of management we've been describing. After working under such leadership on a team or project, people may remark that they were lucky to have been part of something unique, with the unspoken assumption that they may never experience it again. Sometimes even the most able manager may be unable to explain what happened and unsure if she can count on it happening again.

If gifted management is obvious, then why does it seem so elusive? Perhaps it's like catching a butterfly: the instant we do, the beauty and elegance of its flight disappear. And perhaps that's why so much has been written about management with so little improvement in its quality.

We continually hear laments that managers who can lead well are our scarcest commodity. Even businesses with plenty of ideas and capital constantly seek people who can maximize opportunities. The truth, bolstered by our own experiences, is that finding good managers is not hard at all; they have simply been overlooked or underdeveloped. What's needed is not a massive recruiting drive, but simple recognition of the fact that everyone already has within himself the ability to lead. Everyone can access the innate resources—insights, ingenuity, perspective—that fuel progress.

Not the What, Not the How...the Why and "to What End?"

Just as babies come without a manual, most promotions come without a guidebook. It is as if a manager were handed a box of questions the very first day on the job, only to spend the rest of her work life trying to answer them as best she can. While success is expected, there's an unspoken assumption that we will make it on our own, using trial and error to learn the management behaviors that work for us.

Our own experiences were that each step up in responsibility came with at least six months of discomfort, even anxiety. No matter how well we thought we could handle it, the next level always seemed to have a fair share of surprises. No matter how much effort the boss had put into sponsoring us for the new role, we seemed to get little concrete advice once we had it in hand. He or she usually said something along the lines of, "Congratulations, well-deserved, good luck—and if you need any help, just ask." But when you don't even know what it is you don't know, well-meaning but vague offers of assistance do little to stem uncertainty and apprehension.

Promotion is a heady drug. Initially, the new task absorbs us fully. Novelty and adrenaline sweep us forward. Our most urgent questions focus on the substance of managing, the "What do I need to do right now?" or "How can I avoid making a stupid mistake?" But, eventually, the normal stresses of life intrude. The sacrifices of family time, vacations, or personal desires that seemed like investments in our new position now seem endless. New questions may creep in: "Why must I always carry such a heavy load?" and "Is the effort worth it?"

For us, we could not stop at mere management—deployment of people and resources, like moving pieces on a chessboard. Our steps up in responsibility morphed naturally into an impulse to make a positive difference in the life of our organization and in the lives of the people who put their energies to the service of our enterprise. In short, not just to manage, but to lead.

What gives us the right to impact the lives of others? That is what leaders do, as Jack Welch, the celebrated former chairman of General Electric, so clearly articulated. His job, he said, was to "get into the skin of every person so they know their ideas count."[1] All those who have ever managed any group can attest that their intent can be carried out only when others implicitly agree to respond. In other words, leadership requires being true to others as well as to the job at hand. There is a sacred trust whenever we seek to influence the lives of others. Managers who would lead enter into a union whose bonds are those profoundly human qualities of trust, respect, and integrity. Leading is a transcendent act, and a lifelong quest of mastery.

For us, it all comes down to the query "Am I a leader?" Its answer can be revealed only in action—by the process of working and living as if you are actually the leader you aspire to be.

The way to begin is to look within and ask: "What really matters to *me*?" Share your feelings and insights with others, and then explore what is meaningful to *them*. Like a rock dropped into in a pond, your aspiration will create ripples, and those ripples will spread. At some point, statements will begin to emerge and to resonate deeply. Simple words will direct everyone's thoughts toward what really matters. The resulting culture will be grounded in feelings that touch all stakeholders deeply.

What we are pointing to is the fact that we are truly *together* in this game called life. We share the same fundamental human longings—fulfillment, appreciation, joy, accomplishment. And we share the innate resources to satisfy those longings.

Living Our Dreams

The question—"Why lead?"—also serves as the stimulus for releasing leadership in others. But while it is evident to us that everyone has the inborn ability to lead in some way, the issue for too many people is: Will they step forward and do it? Dilettantes, procrastinators, shirkers, and malingerers drain vitality from work groups. But they cannot evade forever the manager who sees through their hesitancy to their underlying fear or insecurity, yet still expects them to step up because he *knows* their secret strength will enable them to take responsibility.

By directing mental energy toward feelings of calm, lightheartedness, humility, integrity, and service, inspiring managers create a workplace where people achieve strong performance on a sustained basis. They establish the tone necessary for peak performance, the trust that underpins collaboration, the reflective time to perceive what is truly needed, and the delegation of responsibility to get the job done. By keeping the question "Why lead?" in mind, you can become a manager who helps others achieve their dreams.

Some people say that dreams are for children. Yet the most successful people have dreamt big dreams. The Wright brothers stepped up from their earthbound bicycle factory to invent the flying machine. Ted Turner saw beyond America's outlook on the "foreign" in creating a world news organization, CNN, which arguably influences more people than any single government. Bill Gates envisioned a PC in every home—a norm accepted 20 fast years later.

Bringing a dream to life is a step-by-step process. Each moment presents us with the possibility of taking action toward our deepest desire. Like a child learning to walk, we may be a bit unsteady at first. But soon we are able to stride with purpose and certainty into the unknown.

Organizations, too, create their own destinies. Great companies, productive teams, or lively organizations are created when people share a common passion—and when their managers have confidence in their innate capacity to make it tangible. While the skilled manager encourages reflection, she also knows that action must be taken every day if dreams are to become tangible. Otherwise, they remain only fleeting thoughts, mere glimmers of possibility.

High-Wire Leadership

Conventional: How To Manage?	Step Up: Why Lead?
"How do I meet goals?"	"What *really* matters to me?"
Carrot and stick get 'em to work harder	"What really matters to *them?*"
Win: big bucks, high praise	"What footprints do I leave behind?"

High-Wire Key to Making It Worth It: Leave "Footprints on the Sands of Time"

Why take on the burden of management? Why brave the high wire?

In other words, what is most important about what we do all day? Why does it matter? In the course of our daily lives, this is not something that we reflect on very much. Who has the time?

Management behaviors—the "how to's"—can be codified, measured, and ranked; they are now routinely used in performance appraisals. But the essential leadership attributes are hidden to the eye; they are about *connection* to others and to the best part of ourselves; they are *spiritual.* "Managers make meaning," consultant and writer David Maister has said.

We are able to help others see that even the biggest dream takes form a step at a time. Reaching for a dream is just like doing anything else; it's a question of putting one foot in front of the other, responding to the changes of each moment.

The ultimate issue is what we leave behind. At the end of our time, will there be anyone to say, "It mattered that they were here?"

> Lives of great men all remind us,
> We can make our lives sublime.
> And, departing, leave behind us
> Footprints on the sands of time.
>
> —Henry Wadsworth Longfellow,
>   "A Psalm of Life" (1839)

Appendix A: Additional Resources

All that ink, all those dead trees. The very number of books on management seems to indicate not only its importance but also its complexity. Management books range from how-to techniques to hagiography.

Leaders have also written books about their own experiences. Personal stories and insights can be memorable; newly promoted managers may well devour such books searching for the secret sauce that they can apply to their situations. But too many former CEOs are hard-pressed to go beyond their own stories, to understand the art of human functioning well enough to help others find it for themselves. This leaves readers struggling to apply these lessons to their own lives.

In our own journeys—from worker to manager, manager to leader; above all, from focus on how to *do* the job to how to *be*—a few books stand out. We refer to them time and again for pragmatic advice, for a better understanding of motivations, for specific tools, for inspiration. Here are a few selections from our bookshelves.

Seeking Pragmatic Advice and Role Models

On Becoming a Leader, by Warren Bennis (Distinguished Professor and Founding Chairman of USC's Leadership Institute)

A wonderful primer that describes the essence of the leadership role in terms of job content.

The Effective Executive, by Peter Drucker (business icon; author of some 30 books over the past 60 years)

The bible on managing and leading that offers practical advice about running organizations. A reference source when one's own knowledge is tapped out.

Good to Great, by Jim Collins (former faculty member at Stanford's Graduate School of Business)

Leaders operate at a hierarchy of competence. The best are paradoxically humble, walking on the path of insight. They use wisdom to accomplish great things in the face of pessimism, doubt, and lousy performance.

Servant Leadership, by Robert K. Greenleaf (essayist who had two careers—at AT&T and in academe, from the Harvard Business School to the Ford Foundation)

A somewhat off-putting title that underscores how radically different a great manager is from those who seek self-aggrandizement or acclaim. The servant leader is the one whose work is based on profound understanding of being human and is so subtle that those being led believe they achieved the results on their own.

Exploring Human Nature to Inform Management

Leadership is an Art and *Leadership Jazz*, by Max DePree (former chairman of Herman Miller)

Two classics written by a CEO who realized that understanding human nature lies at the heart of great leaders.

Sacred Hoops: Spiritual Lessons of a Hardwood Warrior, by Phil Jackson

The renowned basketball coach gives us an insider's look at the higher wisdom of teamwork. He reveals how he links players to their own, clear minds so that they can stay calmly focused in the midst of chaos.

Human Capability: A Study of Individual Potential and Its Application, by Elliot Jacques and Kathryn Cason

A breakthrough book in understanding human capability, intelligence, and development.

What Leaders Really Do, by John Kotter (leadership professor at Harvard Business School)

Kotter describes the basic principles that enable managers to stimulate change, keep focus, get results.

Finding the Meaning That Makes It All Worth It

Synchronicity: The Inner Path, by Joe Jaworski (former litigator; founder of the American Leadership Forum; chairman of Generon Consulting)

Wonderful story of one man's journey to become an enlightened leader and the many miracles that appeared when the results were most in doubt. Inspiring.

Crossing the Unknown Sea: Work as a Pilgrimage of Identity, by David Whyte (poet and business consultant)

Introducing poetry to the workplace as a tool for understanding individual and organizational creativity. Whyte shows that one of the best ways to respond to the call for more effective managers is to overcome our habitual reticence, to bring our fully passionate, creative, human souls right inside the office.

Love & Profit: The Art of Caring Leadership, by James A. Autry (former president of Meredith Magazine Group)

A collection of poems, letters, and essays that explore the emotional and spiritual issues that are the unspoken subtext of every office.

Building Blocks

Unfolding Meaning: A Weekend of Dialogue, by David Bohm

Bohm was one of the greatest physicists and thinkers of the twentieth century. His writings on universal wholeness, connectedness—what has become known as the "holographic paradigm"—are influencing diverse disciplines, including management and teams.

Transitions, by William Bridges (named one of the top-10 executive development presenters in the United States by the *Wall Street Journal*)

Strategies for coping with difficult, painful, and confusing times. Particularly helpful is a way of looking at change that encourages greater comfort with being uncomfortable.

Dialogue with Death: A Journey Through Consciousness, by Eknath Easwaran
    Surprising lessons on living and the sweet promise of answers to life's absorbing questions: Why am I here? Is there a purpose to my life? What happens when I die?

Difficult Conversations: How to Discuss What Matters Most, by Douglas Stone, Bruce Patton, and Sheila Heen (based on 15 years of research at the Harvard Negotiation Project)
    Whether dealing with an unhappy customer or an underperforming employee, the starting point is being able to discern how different perspectives get in the way.

Turning to One Another, by Margaret J. Wheatley (author and organizational consultant)
    As we have said, organizations exist to accomplish things we cannot do alone. Effective managers understand the power of support–given and received. And that begins with "conversations about things that are important."

The Elusive Essence

With all that, there is still an elusive *something*, the intangible essence at the heart of management. For that, we must look beyond accumulated knowledge or experience to the very source of wisdom or gut instinct–our powers of thought. Books in this area include the following.

Illusions: The Adventures of a Reluctant Messiah, by Richard Bach
    A "golden oldie" with a lighthearted approach to a transformational philosophy. When we realize that the origin of what looks absolute is our own thoughts, we break the bonds of limitation.

Slowing Down to the Speed of Life, by Richard Carlson (author of the *Don't Sweat the Small Stuff* series) and psychologist Joseph Bailey
    Speed is the hallmark of contemporary business life. Multitasking, instant messaging. Stress is epidemic. To get relief, we don't have to chuck it all. There is a way to be productive and yet to keep our bearings–to have days that are not only full, but also fulfilling.

Flow: The Psychology of Experience and the Steps Towards Enhancing the Quality of Life, by Mihaly Csikszentmihaly

For more than 25 years, the author has been studying states of "optimal experience," those times when people report feelings of concentration and deep enjoyment. He reveals how this state can be commanded proactively, not just left to chance.

Finally, for those who want to explore thought more deeply in its own right, read *The Missing Link*, by Sydney Banks—a theosopher who knows what he is talking about.

These favorites represent, of course, a small fraction of books about management and leadership. All that noise may mask the truth: anybody can lead well. While management may never be easy, it is actually simple.

In other words, read the books. But also look within.

> We shape ourself
> To fit this world
> And by the world
> Are shaped again.
>
> —David Whyte,
> "Working Together"

Appendix B: Fundamentals

Throughout this book we have pointed to the *innate capacity* to achieve great things without great stress. Underlying our work is a philosophy centered on three powerful intangibles that work together to carry us along, in business and, indeed, in life. They are: *Thought,* which shapes our reality; *Consciousness,* which clarifies our experience of that reality, and *Mind,* which connects us to the universal fabric of life itself. These notions are not new; they have been taught by philosophers, sages, and mystics throughout the ages; they lie at the core of the religions of the world.

Analogies to the ocean help describe the interplay of these principles.

Thought is like the tides, always flowing. As we've seen, we can no more stop our thinking than we can hold back the tides or interrupt an ocean's current. Sometimes our thinking rushes along in a fast surge; at other times, our thoughts meander slowly, like the turning of the tide.

Between flood and ebb tides, the current pauses; that stillness is called "slack water." One of the great engineering feats of the twentieth century—the Golden Gate Bridge—depended on this phenomenon. The current is so strong in and out of San Francisco Bay that the support pilings for the world's most famous suspension bridge could be worked on only twice a day, during the brief release between ebb and flood tides.

You may have experienced slack thinking—moments when mental activity seems to stop, when you may get a sense of the space between thoughts. Indeed, this is the desired calming effect of many meditation practices, as well as prayer. As paradoxical as it may seem, such tranquil moments make possible our greatest productivity.

A second intangible is *Consciousness*: awareness honed moment-by-moment by interaction among senses, feelings, and thoughts. Tranquil, comfortable feelings suggest a tranquil thought process, just as unruffled water points to gentle currents or calm air. Stressful, uncomfortable feelings are signs that our thoughts are like a rapidly moving tidal current, creating turbulence and making it difficult to keep our boat on course. How conscious we are determines how powerfully we lead.

Gaze at the ocean from an airplane at 30,000 feet, and the water looks motionless. We become aware of its force only when we get close enough to see currents flow around objects, to watch boats being tossed by waves, or to hear the surf breaking on the shore. Others are more attuned to the ocean than we. Polynesian sailors found their way to the islands of Hawaii centuries ago, across ₁2,400 miles of ocean without benefit of such tools as sextants and compasses, or even clocks. Instead, they plotted their course by noticing the distinctions in swells, by feel as much as by analysis.

As we navigate through life, our *Consciousness*—the synthesis of sensory feeling and knowing awareness—keeps us attentive and attuned to the dynamic forces moving through and around us each moment.

What powers the oceans' tides? Gravity—the attraction generated by the mass of two bodies, including the pull that connects the orbit of the moon to that of the earth. There is a similar connection at work in human experience— the universal *Mind* common to, and through, all things.

Did you ever stop to wonder where your thoughts come from? We're not speaking about searching for a memory or trying to recall specific facts. That is a function of our brainpower, or intellect. Rather, consider the flashes of insight or inspiration that seem to appear out of nowhere. You're in the shower or driving your car, and they simply come to mind—popping up like kernels in a popcorn maker. Some would say they are products of "original thought," or of the impersonal energy that makes our personal brain function: the universal life force or the spiritual wisdom that exists in every human being. We are all connected to intuition, imagination, Mother Nature, The Way, life force, spirit—the source of energy that is given many names, up to and including God.

Mind, our connection to life itself, is about as well understood as gravity. Scientists can measure and describe gravity's effects in detail—what it does to physical objects. But they cannot tell us how it actually works. Whenever they try to analyze the mechanism of gravity, its essential nature eludes them.

Our connection to the source of our thinking is equally subtle. Neurologists can describe the brain's physiology and functioning, down to the mechanism of electrical charges moving in formation as nerve impulses. They can tell us what structures are involved in certain categories of experience—for example, sensory signals travel to the central nervous system, to specific nuclei in the thalamus in the limbic system, where emotional responses are regulated.

But scientists cannot tell us how personal thought is produced. The reason is simple: *Mind* is a connection to something more fundamental, and at the same time more transcendent, than our intellect. Everyone has a channel to this deep reservoir of universal wisdom. We need only to wait, quietly and without "thinking too much," for insight to emerge from the recesses of our mind.

"All knowledge is just remembering," said Socrates. And he was speaking about all human understanding. Wisdom is the "thought before thought." It's that intuitive leap of understanding that lies just beyond what we can tangibly put into words. All we can do is to accept that our connection to the limitless reservoir of *Mind* impacts our psychological well-being in the same way that we concede gravity's effect on our physical welfare.

Innate Resources

The great news is that these three factors—*Thought, Consciousness*, and *Mind*—are working together all the time, helping to open us to the interconnectedness or oneness of life. They operate like breathing.

Imagine if we had to consciously decide to breathe every second, to command each inhalation and exhalation and then to direct the movement of air to every point within the body that requires oxygen. The effort would demand all of our will, all of our skill; the exertion would be so great that we would never get anything else done.

Luckily, while we have some control over our breathing—we can choose to hold our breath for a time under water, for example—it works on autopilot most of the time. Similarly, *Thought, Consciousness*, and *Mind* act and interact without requiring directed effort. In fact, they work best when we strive to control or contain them least. They are the principles that enable us to recognize, distinguish, and experience life.

> A giant step in becoming an inspirational manager is to comprehend and appreciate:
> . . . that we each have different thoughts, but we all experience a continuous flow of original *Thought*
> . . . that *Consciousness* gives us the awareness to experience our thoughts and feelings with clarity

...that we (and all things) are connected to a universal source of vitality—*Mind*—which constantly makes fresh possibilities available to us

When the Connection Breaks

What happens when the connection between *Thought, Consciousness*, and *Mind* is interrupted? A poignant perspective has been posted on the Web by an autistic adult named Joel (geocities.com/growingjoel).

Joel said that his senses, normally links of *Consciousness*, let him down. His smell, sight, hearing, and touch—all are, Joel said, overly sensitive. They don't do their proper job of shaping attention, guiding his awareness of what's going on in the moment. For example, Joel noted that he has trouble figuring out whether he is hot or cold, hungry or sated. Strong sensations, Joel added, "get me in the most trouble, since they are my body's way of telling me to give attention, but my brain misinterprets them."

Joel deals with his confusion by creating his own mental world, a place where he finds a kind of calm. He plaintively described it as a house, constructed entirely of his own thinking.

Autism is a neurological problem, miscommunication of feeling or body awareness. It's wonderful that Joel has apparently figured out a way around his body miscues. Fortunately, almost all of us have been spared such a neurological problem. But Joel's descriptions inspire a way of looking at *Consciousness*.

Consciousness brings the gift of order and clarity—a lucid sense of our experience. One aspect of *Consciousness* is its role as a counterweight to *Thought*. Without the balancing factor of *Consciousness*, if *Thought* were all we had, none of us could function in a sane way. We could all be like Joel, trapped in our thoughts, cut off from our senses. *Thought* is a constantly flowing steam. *Consciousness* is the ladle that dips down and brings just the right amount of that stream to our lips, where we experience it fully—its coolness, its sweetness. *Consciousness* protects us from being overwhelmed by too many thoughts.

The necessary third leg that ensures balance is the force we are calling *Mind*, which connects us to life itself. Just as *Consciousness* provides us with the clarity to sort *Thought*, so does it allow us to make use of *Mind* by showing us the connections we have to others, to life, and to our own deep wisdom. *Consciousness* is a door that swings both ways, facilitating the interplay of our essential resources, bridging between our individual thoughts and the universal source of all vitality.

As our understanding about this interplay of the three spiritual principles of experience deepens in our own lives, we become more graceful managers. We know that by steering toward connection and by relying more on the wisdom that is always available (even when it is just out of sight), anything we dream of doing is possible. Adversity doesn't throw us off course; stress doesn't move us to overcorrect. We trust our capacity to keep our bearings and to rise above setbacks by shifting our perspective.

Just as a skillful ship's captain knows and understands the ocean's forces, accomplished managers acknowledge the three principles that form human experience. From direct, personal practice, we see the inborn wisdom that every human being possesses. We respect each person's shaping of his own life via thought, and we remain hopeful that all of us can raise our collective understanding so that our lives have more meaning and impact.

> There is a Tide in the affairs of Men,
> Which, taken at the flood, leads on to fortune;
> Omitted, all the voyage of their life
> Is bound in shallows and in miseries.
>
> —*Julius Caesar*, by William Shakespeare

Notes

Introduction: Stepping into the Unknown

1. Cheri Huber, *The Depression Book*, Keep It Simple Books, 1999.
2. *Esquire*, December 1971.

Chapter 1: Grace in Change

1. Client of Gunn Partners, company memorandum, 2002.
2. Henry Ford, *Today and Tomorrow*, p. 8, Doubleday, Page & Company, 1926.

Chapter 2: The Productivity Paradox

1. Promulgated by quality management pioneer, Dr. Joseph Juran, in the 1940s, as the "vital few and trivial many." Also called "Pareto's Principle" after an Italian economist who, in 1906, observed that 80% of the wealth in his country was controlled by 20% of the people.
2. New Ventures West Professional Coaching Course, 2002.
3. philly.com, Sept. 23, 2003.

Chapter 3: Creativity and Strategy

1. Adapted from *Leadership and the New Science*, by Margaret J. Wheatley, Berrett-Kochler Publishers, 1999.

Chapter 4: Better Decisions

1. Taiichi Ohno, *Toyota Production System: Beyond Large-Scale Production*, Cambridge, Mass., Productivity Press, 1988.
2. Quoted in Des MacHale, *Wisdom*, London, 2002.

Chapter 5: Letting Go to Get Ahead

1. One of the best illustrations of this effect is found in Herman Hesse's novel, *Journey to the East*. A group of pilgrims are taking an expedition charted in both spiritual and geographic terms. Their humble servant, Leo, seems to carry everything for them; but Leo leaves the group at a dangerous gorge, where the people begin to argue over their mission. Unable to decide on a common path, the group breaks up, and each pilgrim heads off in his own direction. Only when they return do they see that Leo, the unassuming worker, had actually been their leader. His quiet presence had kept them true to their common pursuit.
2. *New York Times*, July 10, 1998.
3. See, for instance, *Building the Bridge as You Walk On It: A Guide for Leading Change*, by Robert E. Quinn, John Wiley and Sons, 2004.

Chapter 6: Job One—Setting the Right Tone

1. *Harvard Business Review*, February 2004, pp. 22–23.
2. For example, laughter's impact on learning was a hot topic at the 2001 annual conference of the International Association for Supervision and Curriculum Development. The research-based presentation included discussion of "the benefits of integrating humor into brain-based classrooms, including endorphin release and stress reduction." acsd.org.
3. "A Realtor Stays Hot in a Cold Market," *Wall Street Journal*, Jan. 29, 1992.

Chapter 8: Teams—Working as One

1. For further reading on this point, see Jon Katzenbach and Doug Smith, *The Wisdom of Teams*, Harvard Business School Press, 1993.
2. Research tracking the different attitudes of "Generation Y," 18–24 years old, includes the "2002 People at Work Survey" by Mercer Human Resource Consulting. Among the conclusions, a representative told *Georgia Trend Online*: "These workers want mentoring, feedback, access, connection." In addition, Bruce Tulgan of Rainmaker Thinking, a consulting/training firm that closely follows trends among young employees, advises: "The ideal working condition for the youngest workers [the younger the worker, the stronger the trend], is the kind of coaching style relationship with the immediate supervisor, but set in the context of a dynamic team with strong bonds [think Marine Corps]."
3. Phil Jackson and Hugh, Delehanty, *Sacred Hoops*, Hyperion, 1995.
4. Ibid., p. 6.

Chapter 9: Managing Conflict

1. Herbert Simon, *Models of Bounded Rationality*, MIT Press, 1997.
2. Pauline Graham, Editor, *Mary Parker Follett: Prophet of Management*, Harvard Business School Press, 1995.

Chapter 10: Employee Relations

1. When St. John's implemented this employee relations program, it got an un-expected benefit. Management discovered that too many staffers did not understand expected job outcomes; all job training focused on how to perform the work, not how to tell if the work was good. Standards diverged from supervisor to supervisor, causing widespread performance issues and a pervasive sense of unfairness.

Chapter 11: Focus and Clarity

1. Taiichi Ohno, *Toyota Production System: Beyond Large-Scale Production*, Cambridge, Mass., Productivity Press, 1988.
2. "My Idea of Fun," *Fortune* online, Sept. 22, 2003.

Chapter 12: The Antidote to Stress

1. Further explication of this topic can be found in current psychology literature (such as Daniel Goleman's works on "emotional intelligence").
2. *Encyclopaedia Britannica* online; retrieved April 3, 2004.
3. anc.org.
4. Adapted from Jon Kabat-Zinn, *Full Catastrophe Living*, Bantam Dell Publishing Group, Inc., 1990.
5. "Always on the Job, Employees Pay with Health," by John Schwartz, *New York Times*, Sept. 5, 2004.

Chapter 13: Measuring Up

1. Buzzword for quality improvement programs, Six Sigma has been propelled in the late 1990s–early 2000s by such companies as GE. "Why 'Sigma'? The word is a statistical term that measures how far a given process deviates from perfection," it is noted on GE's Web site (ge.com). "The central idea behind Six Sigma is that if you can measure how many 'defects' you have in a process, you can systematically figure out how to eliminate them and get as close to 'zero defects' as possible."

Afterword: Why Lead?

1. Harris Collingwood and Diane L. Coutu, "Jack on Jack," *Harvard Business Review*, Feb. 2002, p. 91.

Index

About the Authors

ROBERT W. GUNN is co-founder of Prescient Leaders, a global leadership development and consulting firm. A pioneer in human resource outsourcing and a long-time executive coach, he created the administrative consulting practice at AT Kearney, and, in 1991, co-founded Gunn Partners, based on the principle of "lean" consulting. With Betsy Gullickson, he writes a monthly column for the executive-level magazine, *Strategic Finance.*

BETSY RASKIN GULLICKSON is an executive coach and communications consultant. Previously, she was a partner at Ketchum, Inc., one of the world's largest PR firms, where she directed the San Francisco business unit and the Global Food & Nutrition Practice. She has also served as a writer/editor at several trade magazines. With Robert Gunn, she writes a monthly column for the executive-level magazine, *Strategic Finance.*